*Deflection/Reflection
In The Lyric Poetry Of Charles d'Orléans*

Scripta humanistica

Directed by
BRUNO M. DAMIANI
The Catholic University of America

ADVISORY BOARD

SAMUEL G. ARMISTEAD
University of California
(Davis)

JUAN BAUTISTA AVALLE-ARCE
University of California
(Santa Barbara)

THEODORE BEARDSLEY
The Hispanic Society of
America

GIUSEPPE BELLINI
Università di Milano

GIOVANNI MARIA BERTINI
Università di Torino

HEINRICH BIHLER
Universität Göttingen

HAROLD CANNON
National Endowment
for the Humanities

DANTE DELLA TERZA
Harvard University

FRÉDÉRIC DELOFFRE
Université de Paris-
Sorbonne

HANS FLASCHE
Universität Hamburg

ROBERT J. DIPIETRO
University of Delaware

GIOVANNI FALLANI
Musei Vaticani

JOHN E. KELLER
University of Kentucky

RICHARD KINKADE
University of Arizona

MYRON I. LICHTBLAU
Syracuse University

JUAN M. LOPE BLANCH
Universidad Nacional Autónoma
de México

LELAND R. PHELPS
Duke University

MARTÍN DE RIQUER
Real Academia Española

JOHN K. WALSH
University of California
(Berkeley)

Deflection/Reflection In the Lyric Poetry Of Charles d'Orléans

A Psychosemiotic Reading

Rouben Charles Cholakian

𝔖cripta humanistica

Publisher and Distributor:
SCRIPTA HUMANISTICA
1383 Kersey Lane
Potomac, Maryland 20854 U.S.A.

The first chapter of this study appeared in modified form in *Fifteenth Century Studies* vol 6 (1983).

© Rouben Charles Cholakian
Library of Congress Catalog Card Number 84-051949
International Standard Book Number 0-9163-79-21-3

Printed in the United States of America

Contents

Introduction: Ambiguities	1
Chapter 1: Perplexed Persona	6
Chapter 2: Syntactical Dynamics	19
Chapter 3: Paradox and Masks	40
Chapter 4: The Closed Circle	59
Conclusion: Signification	79
Appendix A	83
Appendix B	87
Selected Bibliography	89

Introduction
Ambiguities

> Et je, Charles, duc d'Orlians, rimer
> Voulu ces vers. . . .
> (Complainte I, 82–83)

It has been a critical commonplace to cite the name of François Villon as the single most important fifteenth century poet to contribute to the rise of lyric poetry in Europe. But if the comprehensive definition of "lyric" includes poetic preoccupation with self, then one must recognize the equally signficant role of the poet-aristocrat, — contemporary of the more glamorous poet-vagabond Villon, — Charles, Duke of Orléans, whose work in recent years has deservedly come into greater prominence.

Working from opposite ends of the socio-economic hierarchy, and from distinctly different aesthetic and philosophical perspectives, each poet practices self analysis in order to forge a poetic persona, however one might choose to relate that "persona" to its creator. But because of the obliqueness of the allegorical mode, Charles' delineations render his persona more remote, more inaccessible, if not more unreal to the reader.

At one level of analysis, a highly conscious "moi" pointedly engages in the most obvious onomastic identification of self.

> Aux excellens et puissans en noblesse,
> Dieu Cupido et venus la deesse.

> Supplie presentement,
> Humblement,
> Charles, le duc d'Orlians,
> . . . .
> Escript ce jour troisiesme, vers le soir,
> En novembre, ou lieu de Nonchaloir,
> Le bien vostre, Charles, duc d'Orlians,
> Qui jadis fut l'un de voz vrais servans.
> (Songe en complainte, 177–183; 547–545)[1]

While N. L. Goodrich sees in this bombastic self-identification "a general current perceivable throughout the century and linked to a growing realization in art of the individual *per se*," she also notes significantly that Charles "suffered from the handicap of being the son of a world-famous father who had been the regent and actual ruler of France."[2] She thus hints at the potential psychological implications of this need to name oneself, suggesting that the issue is perhaps more complex than is at first apparent.

Indeed, even the most desultory reading of the Charles d'Orléans text gives evidence of a basic and unmistakable contradiction in the persona's self-image. On the one hand, an analytical "moi" devotes inordinate energies to defining his emotions:

> Que voulez vous que je vous die?
> Je suis pour ung asnyer tenu,
> Banny de Bonne Compaignie,
> et de Nonchaloir retenu (Ballade, 117)

Yet, on the other, that same "moi" frequently speaks of withdrawal:

> Tout a part moy, en mon penser m'enclos,
> Et fais chasteaulz en Espaigne et en France;
> Oultre lez montz forge mainte ordonnance,
> Chascun jour j'ay plus de mille propos,
> En mez pais, quant me treuve a repos. (Rondeau, 54)

---

[1] All references are to the Pierre Champion edition, *Charles d'Orléans: Poésies*, 2 vols (1923–27; reprinted, Paris: Honoré Champion, 1975).
[2] *Charles d'Orléans: A Study of Themes in His French and in His English Poetry* (Geneva: Droz, 1967), p. 35. In her own analysis of the question, Alice Planche views the onomastic tendency as the self-awareness of both artist and aristocrat. *Charles d'Orléans ou à la recherche d'un langage*. (Paris: Honoré Champion, 1975), p. 680.

Charles creates an ambiguous persona whose poetic vision is turned both inwards and outwards, a "moi" for whom *écriture* is both identification and mask, self-definition and subterfuge, *reflection* and *deflection*. As Alice Planche puts it, " 'Je' n'est ni fidèle à lui-mème, ni simple."[3]

This dialectic of deflection/reflection becomes, moreover, a fundamental key to interpreting the message of a persona who defines, conceals and even, on occasion, plays at being self. The Charles d'Orléans poetry, in brief, is prototypical of text in general, where poetic discourse is always both mystery and clarification: "L'oeuvre est tout ensemble une fermeture et un accès, un secret et la clé de son secret.[4]

Traditional psychocritical examination of text deals with such ambiguities by an analytical process which tries to search for the creative persona not only in the more transparent descriptions of "moi" but in the reality which lies buried beneath the textual signs, both conscious and unconscious:

> Dès l'instant où nous admettons que toute personnalité comporte un inconscient, celui de l'écrivain doit être compté comme source hautement probable de l'oeuvre.[5]

Although Sigmund Freud himself did not personally devote a major part of his psychoanalytical energies to literary criticism, his interest in the language of the unconscious inevitably led him to conjecture that one could deal with the manifest content of the creative expression in much the same way he dealt with the apparent message of the dream sequence:

> ...les rêves inventés par un écrivain sont susceptibles des mêmes interprétations que les rêves réels, donc que, dans l'activité créatrice du poète, les mêmes mécanismes de l'inconscient du rêve entrent en jeu qui nous sont déjà connus par le travail d'élaboration du rêve.[6]

---

[3] *Charles d'Orléans ou à la recherche d'un langage*, p. 678.
[4] Jean Rousset, *Forme et signification* (Paris: José Corti, 1962), p. ii.
[5] Charles Mauron, *Des Métaphores obsédantes au mythe personnel* (Paris: José Corti, 1964), p. 31.
[6] Sigmund Freud, *Ma Vie et la psychanalyse* (Paris: Gallimard, 1968), p. 81.

Freud engendered, thus, a whole new attitude toward the created word. Since his time, literary theorizing has given an important place to the "subtext," to the latent content of what is being said, to the underlying language spoken by the unconscious, to the text as the "véhicule d'une parole, en tant qu'elle constitue une émergence nouvelle de la vérité."[7]

Most studies of this type, however, tend to focus almost exclusively upon thematic elements to the neglect of the syntagm. They limit themselves to the signifiers but do not examine their syntactical relationships. And yet, if one does accept the fundamental premise that unconscious reality exists, it should follow logically that any serious psychosemiotic interpretation must deal as much with the syntagm as with the lexeme of the poetic discourse, for the "significance" of the text is by definition all-encompassing:

> From the standpoint of meaning the text is a string of successive information units. From the standpoint of significance the text is one semantic unit. Any sign within that text will therefore be relevant. . . .[8]

Consequently, two principles guide the present study:

1. Textual signs communicate more than the manifest denotative message.
2. Syntagm and lexeme are inseparable constituents of the same semiotic unit.

With this therefore as a general statement of methodology, we shall proceed to examine the lyrical works of Charles d'Orléans, first the ballades, and then the rondeaux.[9] We shall in each case

---

[7] Jacques Lacan, *Ecrits* (Paris: Seuil, 197), p. 381. For reviews of the history of both psychological and psychoanalytical influences on critical methods, one can profitably consult: Joseph P. Strelka, ed., *Literary Criticism and Psychology* (University Park, Pa.: Pennsylvania State University Press, 1976); J. Le Galliot, *Psychanalyse et langages littéraires: théorie et pratique* (Paris: F. Nathan, 1977); and Pamela Tytell, *La Plume sur le divan: psychanalyse et littérature en France* (Paris: Aubier Montaigne, 1982).

[8] Michael Riffaterre, *Semiotics of Poetry* (Bloomington, Indiana: University Press, 1978), p. 3.

[9] We shall not attempt to deal here with the so-called "English poetry" sometimes attributed to Charles d'Orléans, inasmuch as its authenticity continues to be in doubt. Speaking of these poems, David Fein has written recently: "Much

cull out the psychological signification of textual signs and then look for corroborative syntagmatic features, most particularly in the refrain structures. The hope is, that this careful use of modern psychocritical tools will in some measure provide a more complete and therefore more accurate portrait of this complex poetic persona who paradoxically indulges in seemingly candid self-examination, but also seeks asylum behind the protective mechanisms of literary expression, this poetic persona who sometimes identifies himself as "je, Charles, duc d'Orlians..."[10]

investigation remains to be done in this area, and a definite conclusion may never be reached. Until such time as this mystery is solved, the English poetry will remain a fascinating enigma." *Charles d'Orléans* (Boston: Twayne, 1983), p. 87.

[10] Aside from the brief article by David Fein, in which he deals only with Ballade 36 ("Verb Usage in a Ballad of Charles d'Orléans," *Romance Philology*. XXXV [November: 1981], no one has attempted a syntactical, let alone a thorough psychosemiotic study of Charles' poetry. Although Alice Planche's impressive work *(Charles d'Orléans ou à la recherche d'un langage)*, represents a perceptive reading of the poetic imagery, it barely touches upon fundamental issues of syntax. As Daniel Poirion remarks in his review of the Planche study: "On ne relève que très peu de remarques sur la syntaxe, alors qu'une des caractéristiques essentielles de la poésie lyrique est la tension qu'établit une versification rigoureuse avec l'expansion normale de la phrase." *Romania* 99 (1978), p. 556.

Chapter 1
Perplexed Persona

> Folie et Sens me gouvernent tous deux.
> (Ballade 120)

Through the poetic conventions of the "allegorical mode"[1] the persona of the ballade engages in an intriguing and untiring auto-critique, in a dialectic between anxiety and hope, deflection and reflecton.

On occasion, the persona appears to argue with himself, to urge himself to take up the "avirons d'Espoir" so as not to stagnate in "l'eau de Fortune si quoye." (93) More frequently, however, he concludes that the correct course of action is retreat in the face of "Dangier." Instead of acting as aggressor, he prefers to draw back.

How, for example, does he react, when Dame Fortune boasts, in the well-known series of "Fortune" ballades, of her power over helpless, victimized humanity?

> Car, quant aucuns en mes mains prens,
> D'en bas je les monte en haultesse

---

[1] Following her careful analysis of the rhetoric in Charles' poetry, Anne Tukey Harrison concludes that "what might have seemed to be full allegory is actually the allegorical mode, pseudo-allegory, or allegory-like writing." *Charles d'Orléans and the Allegorical Mode* (Chapel Hill: University of North Carolina Press, 1975), p. 118.

> Et d'en hault en bas les descens,
> Monstrant que suis Dame et maistresse,... (113)

Instead of a vigorous defense, one hears the feeble, unsure and wavering voice of the persona timidly echo:

> Souventesfoiz, contre raison,
> Boutez de hault plusieurs en bas
> Et de bas en hault; telz debas
> Vous usez en vostre maison. (114)

And as if this quiet resignation to mistreatment were not enough, the cowering "moi" gives way to strident self-deprecation: "On me deust bien, sans flaterie,/Chastier, despoillié tout nu... (117)[2]

What is more, this morose self-censureship seems to provoke incurable, psychosomatic disorders:

> Guerir ne se puet maladie
> Par phisique, ne cireurgie,
> Astronomians n'enchanteurs,
> Des maulx que seuffrent povers cueurs
> Par le vent [de Merencolie]. (111)

Allegorical enemies gather around the plagued persona, pursue it, hold it prisoner, and force it to wear a mask of compliant pleasantness:

> Quant je deusse bonne chiere
> Demener en compaignie,
> Je n'en fais que la maniere:
> Car quoy que ma bouche rie,
> Du parle parolle lye,
> Dangier et destresse fiere
> Boutent monplaisir arriere;
> Je pry Dieu qu'il les maudie! (25)

And so the "moi" inhabits the darkness of "boys de Merencolie" (43), suffers from "fievre... de merencolie" (107), sees himself as inescapably "deffie... de Merencolie et douleur." (99) Mind and body together bear the intolerable weight of a crushing and

---

[2] One is tempted to compare these remarks with Villon's where the tone, however, is far less self-destructive. Cf. *Le Grand Testament*, the *huitains* XXII–XXVI.

debilitating insecurity. The love imagery, while it conforms to the customary courtly topology: idealized female, incomparable suffering of the lover, torn between desire and frustration, expectancy and hesitation, suggests also anxieties at a much deeper, psychological level.[3] The created "moi", poet-lover, would like to believe that love (faith) can defeat death (fear):

> Quant Pitié vit que franchement
> Voulu mon cueur abandonner
> Envers ma Dame, tellement
> Traitta que lui fist me laisser
> Son cueur, me chargeant le garder,
> Dont j'ay fait mon loyal devoir,
> Maugré Dangier, qui recevoir
> M'a fait chascun jour de telz tours
> Que sans mort en ce point manoir
> Ce n'est que miracle d'Amours. (20)

But that desperate hope is constantly threatened by the image of Death: "C'est grant peril de regarder/Chose dont peut venir la mort;" (3) There in the beckoning eye of Amours, the anxious "moi" perceives the threat of annihilation: "Je croy que me voulez tuer." (5) The cautious oversensitized self therefore seems to pull away from potential, new suffering:

> De jamais n'amer par amours
> J'ay aucune fois le vouloir,
> Pour les ennuieuses dolours
> Qu'il me fault souvent recevoir;... (7)

The same kind of ambivalence is manifested toward friendship. The fragile ego requires the assurance and solace of loyalty. In time of distress, the "moi" solicits the quick and reassuring response of allies: "Au feu, au feu, courez tous mes amis!" (26) It projects onto sympathetic on-lookers the compassion it so longs for itself: "Lors vissiez mes amis pleurer,/Quant sceurent le point ou j'estoye;...(99) More concretely, when Charles speaks of his "gracieux cousin" and "compaignon treschier," the Duc de Bourbon,

---

[3] "Mais comme l'amour représente la vie dans son intensité, ce qui l'interdit est signe et symbole de tout abandon." Planche, *Charles d'Orléans ou à la recherche d'un langage*, p. 608.

he demands nothing less than the unflinching devotion characterized by the ancient feudal code of "Compagnage": "Or y faictes comme j'ay la fiance,/Car un amy doit pour l'autre veillier." (83) The poet in turn of course promises the same:

> Qui m'ostera de ce tourment.
> Il m'achetera plainement
> A tousjours més, a heritage:
> Tout sien seray, sans changement.
> [Mettroye] corps et ame en gage! (93)

But alas, Charles is nonetheless unrelentingly tormented by fears of defection and breach of trust. These are more than the natural suspiciousness of a political prisoner wary of conspiracy and betrayal. In the special psychological context we have been describing, terms such as "loyal, loyaument, loyaulté, faulx and faulceté," so all-pervasive in the ballades, assume a significance which goes beyond the bounds of the allegorical language of courtly traditions.[4] If the poet places such emphasis on the qualities of trust and loyalty, it is precisely because the hurtful consequences of earlier deceptions have caused him to be circumspect. To his cousin the duke he says,

> Et sans plus desprendre langage,
> A cours mots, plaise vous penser
> Que vous laisse mon cueur en gage
> Pour tousjours, sans jamais faulser. (88)

In spite of his misgivings, he longs to trust in the curative effects of love:

> Aydiez moy a l'outrecuidance
> Vengier, com en vous ay fiance
> Ma Maistresse, je vous supply,
> De ce faulx Dangier qui m'avance
> Dieu scet en quel mauvais party. (22)

---

[4] Daniel Poirion already greatly expands the implications of the topos: "...on devine d'autres préoccupations que celles de la fidelité amoureuse. Loyalisme politique, foi chrétienne semblent interférer avec la donnée traditionnelle de l'amour courtois." *Le Lexique de Charles d'Orléans dans les ballades* (Geneva: Droz, 1967), p. 94.

He would like to endorse the reality of a "paradis de amoureux," but "Dangier . . . ce faulx traistre, vilain, hideux" torments the "moi" who gropes toward some sense of peace and security and plunges himself anew "Ou purgatoire de Tristesse." (24)

"Dangier" takes on the aspect of a spying intruder, ubiquitous, awesome and terrifying, from whom the poet tries in vain to escape:

> Et se mettra souvent en presse
> D'ouir tout ce que je diray
> Mais je pense que par sagesse
> Si tresbien me gouverneray
> Et telle maniere tendray
> Que faulx Dangier trompé sera,
> Ne nulle riens n'appercevra;
> Si mettra il sa painne toute
> D'espier tout ce qu'il pourra;
> C'est une chose que fort doubte. (51)

In the end, the protective mechanisms of the human psyche must intervene to shelter the injured self. The vulnerable ego must withdraw into a comfortable retreat from reality. Metaphorically, in the ballades, this phenomenon expresses itself in the critical motif of *distance*, distance first from the external realities which are a part of the creator's psychological make-up.[5]

Enough has probably already been said on the theme of "Nonchaloir" as the personification of Charles' introversion into the sanctuary of his private, emotional life.[6] But what is perhaps less often pointed out is the strange ambivalence of the poetic persona's attitude toward that supposedly comforting asylum.

The "moi" speaks reassuringly about having "tout mis a nonchaloir." (7) He hopes to find solace in some sort of stoic

---

[5] For an interesting review of the question of poetic distance see Sergio Cigado, *L'Opera poetica di Charles d'Orléans* (Milano: Vita et Pensiero, 1960), pp. 163–167.

[6] At least two studies have dealt specifically with this important topos: Constanza Pasquali, "Charles d'Orléans e il suo 'Nonchaloir.'" in *Studi in onore de Angelo Monteverdi* (Paris: Nizet, 1974), and more recently, Shigemi, Sasaki, *Sur le Thême de Nonchaloir dans la poésie de Charles d'Orléans* (Paris: Nizet, 1974).

resignation,[7] not having discovered it in the pursuit of love:"Pour ce je metz du tout a nonchaloir." (18) And to some extent he can in fact boast that "L'emplastre de Noncnhaloir ... m'a guery." (73) But another part of the persona cries out just as emphatically: "Ne me mettez a nonchaloir / Honte sera se me failliés." (52) He speaks disparagingly, what is more, of the thought of "Portant harnoys rouillé de Nonchaloir." (108) He repeats the idea in the famous Ballade 72,

> Essaier vueil se je sauroye
> Rimer ainsi que je souloye.
> Au meins j'en feray mon povoir,
> Combien que je congnois et sçay
> Que mon langage trouveray
> Tout enrouillié de Nonchaloir.

And again in the crucial Ballade 117 he writes:

> Que voulez vous que je vous die?
> Je suis pour ung asnyer tenu,
> Banny de Bonne Compaignie,
> Et de Nonchaloir retenu
> Pour le servir. Il est conclu!

These poetic statements are not only expressions of painful confrontations with the passage of time, but suggest earlier psychic wounds which lead the persona to be cautious and fearful.

This psychological interpretation seems reinforced by the significant fact that while "Nonchaloir" represents the abstract conceit in allegorical form, the ballades offer evidence also of numerous concrete images to express this anxiety. Throughout the poetry appears a whole series of images denoting retreat into protective enclosures of one sort or another which can save the delicate ego from further assaults. At one moment, for example, the poetic "moi" notes,

> Je ne crains Dangier ne les siens,
> Car j'ay garny la forteresse

---

[7] "Prendre tout pour un jeu, c'est une façon de voir l'infime et le suprême degré de Nonchaloir (le non-sérieux et le sérieux)." Sasaki, *Sur le Thème de nonchaloir*, p. 213.

> Ou mon cueur a retrait ses biens,
> De Reconfort et de Lyesse; ... (29)

At another he speaks of being "enveloppé / En ung cueuvrechief de Plaisance."(32) He delights in thinking of himself as protected in his "hermitage de Pensee." (43) In a similar vein he writes: "Lors la chambre de ma pensee / De grant plaisance reluira." (45) In the much-quoted Ballade 105, one reads of an imaginary voyage "En la forest de Longue Actente" wherein the travelor finds lodgings in "l'ostellerie de Pensee." In yet another journey, the "moi" looks forward to bringing his "galee ... chargee de marchandise / De mainte deverse pensee" to safe harbor. (109) In all of these cases the poet introduces images which underscore his need for withdrawal into a private and safe retreat, a subconscious return to the womb where he cannot be harmed by the disappointments of rejection. Unlike Montaigne's "arrière-boutique," this inner sanctuary is more psychological than intellectual in nature, more emotional than cerebral.

But herein lies the paradox, for such a retreat from the possible hurt of future encounters brings the poet into direct contact with the recollections of past hurts:

> Le beau souleil, le jour saint Valentin
> Qui apportoit sa chandelle alumee,
> N'a pas long temps, entra un bien matin
> Priveement en ma chambre fermee.
> Celle clarté, qu'il avoit apportee,
> Si m'esveilla du somme de Soussy
> Ou j'avoye toute la nuit dormy
> Sur le dur lit d'Ennuieuse Pensee. (66)

Thus, to realize a safe distance from the "somme de Soussy" born of reflection, "Sur le dur lit d'Ennuieuse Pensee," the poet must interpose a *second* poetic persona between himself, the creator and observer, and the inner self, the subject of analysis. That second created persona is called here the "cueur."[8] Let us take a closer look at how this psychological phenomenon functions in the text.

[8] "...cueur n'est pas une personne distincte, il n'est pas incarné.... L'emploi de ce terme permet de s'étudier à la troisième personne, avec plus d'objectivité, et plus d'écho." (Planche, *Charles d'Orléans ou à la recherche d'un langage*) "By fragmenting his personality in two distinct entities...the poet partially dissociates

On occasion, "cueur" resembles a close friend, ready to give solace and advice. When troubled by his twin enemies "Merencolie" and "Douleur" the "moi" seeks the counsel of "Les Trois Estas de mon cueur," and himself proffers comfort to others by assuring them that "Bon remede je trouveroye / Par les Trois Estas de mon cueur." (99) Similarly, he speaks of holding council "En la Chambre de ma pensee," where his "cueur . . . faisoit appareil / De deffence contre l'armee / De fortune." (118) In any event, distance is realized by the fact that "cueur" maintains a separate identity quite apart from that of the narrating, analytical "moi" or first persona. But, curiously, like psychic mirrors, the poetic self and this second created self often share each others' mutual distress:

> Car, ainsi qu'a present je n'ay
> En mon cueur que dueil et tourment
> Il est aussi pareillement
> Troublé, plain de vent et de pluie; . . . (53)

The confusing paradox of distinct identities co-habiting within a single psyche persists throughout the poetic auto-analysis of the ballades. This psychological mechanism bears resemblance thus to the concept of the "split personality," one of the well-known classic symptoms of the patient seeking retreat from trauma.[9]

In even the earliest love ballades,[10] the persona speaks of going to see "mon cueur, tout secrettement." (6) In another, he writes: "L'autr'ier alay mon cueur veoir,/Pour savoir comment se portoit." (37) The secret personality is the recipient of good news as well as bad:

> Sitost que l'autre jour j'ouy
> Que ma souveraine sans per
> Estoit guerie, Dieu mercy,

---

himself from the emotional conflict represented by the *prison de Desplaisance*" (Fein, *Charles d'Orléans*, p. 27).

[9] One should not confuse the issue by thinking of the popularized and over-simplified uses of this term as represented in literary works such as *Dr. Jekyll and Mr. Hyde*.

[10] We are accepting the approximate chronology established by Cigado who situates the composition of Ballades I–CXIV between the years 1415–1440 and the remaining in the period between 1448–1458.

> Je m'an alay sans point tarder
> Vers mon cueur pour le lui conter. (56)

In Ballade 119 the initial "moi" even offers counsel to this second personality called "cueur":

> A mon cueur je conseille lors
> Qu'i prenons nostre demouree,
> Et que par nous soit bien gardee
> Contre tous ennuyeux rappors.

The relationship fluctuates between domination on one side or the other, like some sort of emotional see-saw. On occasion, for example, the exteriorized creative self defines the psychic distress in terms of an invisible domination from within:

> Mais en la fin, pour dire voir,
> Quelque mal que doye porter,
> Je vous asseure, par ma foy,
> Que je n'en sauroye garder
> Mon cueur qui est maistre de moy. (7)

Ballade 74 begins: "Mon cueur m'a fait commendment / De venir vers vostre jeunesse."

But more often the poet's metaphorical construct places the second persona or "cueur" in the psychological posture of victim, as the poet-analyst surveys himself at a safe distance, emotionally detached, as it were, from his own reality:

> Trop long temps vous voy sommeillier,
> Mon cueur, en dueil et desplaisir;
> Vueilliez vous, ce jour, esveillier:
> Alons au bois le may cueillir,
> Pour la coustume maintenir. (48)

Upon the news of the death of his wife, Bonne d'Armagnac, the "moi" prefers, once more, to deflect the pain onto the other self:

> N'en parlons plus: mon cueur se pasme
> Quand il oyt les faist vertueux
> D'elle, qui estoit sans nul blasme.... (69)

In sum, reflection *within* self invariably leads to deflection *from* self; that appears to be the repeated psychological fact in the ballades. And what does it tell us about the persona?

In any interpretation of the ballades, it is of course entirely possible to go no further than either the allegorical message of love or, for that matter, the immediate socio-historical context in which one might situate the poetic language of Charles d'Orléans. But there are compelling arguments to place the poetic symbols in their broader psychological framework, to view the metaphoric language of the courtly idiom as an invitation to look behind the textual signs, in a word, to decode the latent meaning, for that other message is there, whether or not the poet realizes it: "Charles d'Orléans s'est pourtant constitué une sorte de code, peut-être sans le vouloir, mais non sans le savoir."[11]

Moreover, the obliqueness of allegory lends itself to this kind of psychological interpretation, one which presupposes a deciphering technique:

[Psychological analysis] rend moins désuet l'usage des métaphores et des allégories comme moyen de définition et d'approche d'une réalité qui échappe à l'analyse logique.[12]

But what in fact is the latent message? How must one finally read the allegorical and metonymic reductions? What, in the end, is the psychic code of the textual displacement of poetic metaphor?[13]

The key, it would seem, is the important relationship

---

[11] Planche, *Charles d'Orléans ou à la recherche d'un langage*, p. 13.

[12] *Charles d'Orléans ou à la recherche d'un langage*, p. 728. C. G. Jung made essentially the same observation when he noted that poetic symbols are often "the best possible expression for an unconscious content whose nature can only be guessed." It is John Fox who quotes Jung here and then goes on to say: "The very imprecision of his imagery made Charles take a step away from allegory in the direction of impressionism and symbolism. In other words, he moved away from a conscious paraphrase whose scope was clearly delimited, towards a more general evocation in which suggestion took the place of definition." *The Lyric Poetry of Charles d'Orléans* (Oxford: Clarendon Press, 1969), pp. 74–75. Planche also remarks: " 'L'impressionisme' convient à la prise de conscience nerveuse, qui aboutit à une acuité sans éclat, comme des cris en sourdine." *Charles d'Orléans ou à la recherche d'un langage*, p. 727. And Daniel Poirion writes: "Nous ne sommes plus dans le verger du *Roman de la Rose* ou les images sont disposées selon le plan rigoureux du didactisme. Avec Charles d'Orléans la poésie propose déjà au lecteur: '. . . des forêts de symboles / Qui observent avec des regards familiers.' " *Le Poète et le prince: l'évolution du lyrisme courtois de Guillaume de Machaut à Charles d'Orléans* (Paris: Presses universitaires de France, 1965), p. 613.

[13] Le Galliot, *Psychanalyse*, pp. 63–67.

established between the "moi" and the second invented persona identified as "cueur." One readily recognizes here a psycholiterary device which renders less painful communication between the conscious and the wounded, hidden self. "Cueur," in other words, is a psychological projection, a fragmentation of self, and, as such, not unrelated to the Lacanian concept of the Other:

> L'Autre est donc le lieu où se constitue le je qui parle avec celui qui entend, ce que l'un dit étant déjà la réponse et l'autre décidant à l'entendre si l'un a ou non parlé.[14]

The poetic language of the ballade, thus, describes an inner conflict metaphorized in the special psychic kinship of "moi"and the projected self called "cueur," and decodable via the manifest discourse of the courtly dialogue.

A psychological reading of the ballades reveals in metaphorical language a persona frightened by love and, at the same time, eagerly in search of the security born of loyalty and affection. It shows an anxious persona reaching out to the world around and at the same time paradoxically withdrawing from it. It describes, in brief, a profoundly traumatized psyche: "Même pour un seigneur d'un temps déchiré, sa biographie est exceptionellement tragique."[15]

It is possible thus to identify here many of the classical symptoms associated with the introverted personality, as analyzed by C. G. Jung:

1. [The introvert] is terrified of strong affects in others and is hardly ever free of the dread of falling under hostile influences.
2. Anything strange and new arouses fear and mistrust, as though concealing unknown perils.

---

[14] Lacan, *Ecrits*, p. 431.
[15] Planche, *Charles d'Orleans où à la recherche d'un langage*, p. 161. His successful father Louis fell at the hands of political assassins when Charles was barely fourteen. (1407) Too young for the charge laid upon him, Charles, moreover, had none of the natural charisma or leadership qualities possessed by his more gregarious father. Within a year of his father's brutal murder, he witnessed the death of a doting mother no longer able to bear her own inconsolable grief. (1408) And one short year later, Charles lost his young bride Isabelle. As for his second wife, Bonne d'Armagnac, Charles scarcely knew her when suddenly he was taken prisoner at Agincourt (1415). Worse still, she died prematurely before his release from twenty-five years as a political prisoner in England.

3. His ideal is a lonely island where nothing moves except what he permits to move.[16]

Throughout the ballades, one encounters the persistent presence of "Dangier," and a nearly obsessive preoccupation with "loyauté." In his desperate quest for acceptance and love, the persona becomes a prisoner of the haunting fear of new rejections. He is pursued by the ugly grimace of "Merencolie,"[17] and seeks retreat into the "lonely island" of his "chambre de pensee," his inner "forteresse," "where nothing moves except what he permits to move." The poet creates in this fashion a protective space between his public and private personae.

Poetry permits him to escape briefly from the anguish of the world of cruel frustrations and unjust burdens for which he feels himself eminently unprepared. But there, in the inner recesses of his "chambre de pensee," he must struggle with an overriding *self*-condemnation, the nagging sense of debilitating inadequacy. Twenty-five long years of incarceration represent for him not only a humiliating emasculation but a cosmological pronouncement upon his own deficiencies:

> Fruit suis d'hyver qui a meins de tendresse
> Que fruit d'esté; si suis en garnison,
> Pour amolir ma trop verde duresse,
> Mis pour meurir ou feurre de prison! (80)

The semi-facetious tone adumbrates the fear of never in fact reaching maturity, worse still, an abiding guilt for not wishing to. The imprisonment, in sum, is psychological, since Charles cannot escape hating and loving what he is.[18]

To come to terms with the conflict of his warring nature,

---

[16] "Psychological Types," in *The Portable Jung* (New York: Penguin Press, 1976), p. 236.
[17] "Pour nous, 'Mélancolic' a toute une gamme d'acception, depuis le sens clinique jusqu'à une vague tristesse." (Planche, *Charles d'Orléans ou à la recherche d'un langage*, p. 600.
[18] "The prisoner in England was fond of presenting himself as a prisoner of love, and later he depicted himself as the prisoner of old age. In fact he was above all the prisoner of his own self, unable to escape from his forlorn personality, able to forget it only for the occasional brief moment." Fox, *The Lyric Poetry of Charles d'Orléans*, p. 74.

Charles employs to his own advantages the distance already inherent in the allegorical mode of expression. He infuses the old style with a new intimacy, but at the same time, turns *poetic* into *psychological* distance by stepping aside to examine his afflicted "cueur" as if it were indeed someone else's and he merely the objective poet-analyst. In this manner, he creates a psycho-poetic drama in which the projected "moi" serves as a distancing device, transforming the *reflective* discourse into a psychologically *deflective* tactic.

If this is the fundamental signification to be gleaned from a topological review of the ballades of Charles d'Orléans, it remains to be seen whether a syntagmatic analysis corroborates these important conclusions about the persona, and to that question we now turn our attention.

Chapter 2
Syntactical Dynamics

> L'autre jour tenoit son conseil
> En la chambre de ma pensee
> Mon cueur qui faisoit appareil
> De deffence contre l'armee
> De Fortune, mal advisée
> Qui guerryer vouloit Espoir
> Se sagement n'est reboutee
> Par Bon Eur et Loyal Vouloir
> (Ballade 118)

An exhaustive review of all the syntagmatic features of the poetry of Charles d'Orléans would be an awesome undertaking. The present analysis will consider only one important aspect of syntactical dynamics, the ballade refrain.

Although modern criticism has dealt with defining the role of Charles d'Orléans ballade refrain in terms of the general transition towards a more personalized kind of lyric, that analysis has confined itself for the most part to thematic considerations.[1]

---

[1] For general studies on form, one might profitably consult the following basic works: Fr. Gennrich, *Grundriss einer Formenlehre des mittelalterlichen Liedes also Grundlage einer musikalischen Formenlehre des Liedes* (Halle: Saale,

Crucial questions of form and precisely how the syntactical interdependence of refrain and stanza might also relate to that development remain essentially unexplored.[2]

What, if any, is the link between refrain and stanza? Is the poet consistent from stanza to stanza? Does he show any preferences? Do any patterns emerge, any identifiable evolution? Finally, can one discern any meaningful relationship between form and content as regards the use of the refrain in the ballades of Charles d'Orléans?

One ought no doubt to begin with a clear definition of terms. What is to be understood by "syntactical" in this context? Unless the refrain stands as a distinct, grammatical unit separated by a period, a semi-colon, or, as it sometimes happens in pre-classical punctuation practices, a colon,[3] the refrain is *syntactically linked to what precedes*.[4] With that as a working definition, let us now try to identify the functions of the ballade-refrain in Charles d'Orléans.

1932); Hans Spanke, *Beziehungen zwischen romanischer und mittellateinischer Lyrik mit besonderer Berücksichtigung des Metrik und Musik* (Berlin; Abhandlung des Gesellschaft der Wissenschaft zu Göttingen, 1936); Georges Lote, *Histoire du vers français*. 3 vols., (Paris: Boivin, 1949–55); Roger Dragonetti, *La Technique poétique des trouvères dans la chanson courtoise* (Bruges: De Tempel, 1960); Paul Zumthor, *Langue et techniques poétiques à l'époque romane* (Paris: Klincksieck, 1963); and Gilbert Reaney, "Concerning the Origins of the Rondeau, Virelai and Ballade Forms," *Musica Disciplina* VI (1952): 155–166. And of course to this should be added the excellent pages devoted to structure in Poirion's thorough and intelligent review of form, *Le Poète et le prince*, pp. 311–480.

[2] One is inevitably reminded of the call to arms of Roman Jakobson: "... bref, la poésie de la grammaire et son produit littéraire, la grammaire de la poésie, ont été rarement reconnues par les critiques et presque totalement négligées par les linguistes." *Essai de linguistique générale* Trad. by N. Ruwet (Paris: Edition de Minuet, 1963), p. 224. Although John Fox speaks intelligently about the general structure of the ballade, he says nothing about the refrain itself. *The Lyric Poetry*, pp. 106–115. Daniel Poirion's own pertinent remarks are essentially thematic. *Le Poète et le prince*, pp. 394–95.

[3] See U. T. Holmes and Alexander Schutz, *A History of the French Language* (Columbus, Ohio: Harold Hedrick, 1948), pp. 88–89.

[4] We have excluded from our analysis the occasional "envoi" since, as Dragonetti notes: "Come tel, l'envoi, n'était pas une partie indispensable du grand chant courtois...," *La Technique*, p. 306.

The Non-syntactical Refrain

One immediately notes that there exist a certain number of ballades (4, 6, 8, 25, 40, 41, 51, 59, 74, 83, 91, 108)[5] which stand grammatically alone.

In Ballade 6, for example, the poet provokes a heated debate with "cueur," traditional confidant of his innermost feelings and dispenser of courtly advice. In each of the three structurally parallel stanzas, "cueur" concludes his remarks at the penultimate verse, leaving the refrain to serve as a kind of quintessential reduction, or metaphoric *précis* of what has gone before: "Ainsi m'ont raporté mes yeulx."

In Ballade 26, one finds much the same phenomenon. The refrain serves as a dramatic evocation which heightens the emotional pitch of the theme with a powerful and histrionic final gesture: "Je l'oy crier piteusement secours."

On occasion, the poet resorts to a more violent explosion of emotion in which punctuation reinforces the psychological content. Such is the case, for example, in Ballade 40 where the refrain of the second stanza divides into an abrupt expletive followed quickly by a pert and ironic question: "Helas! et n'est ce pas assez?"

One encounters a somewhat different procedure in Ballade 76. The key word "priez" begins the stanza and then in litany fashion reappears in each of the refrains: "Priez pour paix, le vray tresor de joye!" The poet's supplications gain in dramatic intensity in a refrain whose emotional impact is derived from the very way it is linked syntactically to the rest of the stanza. It is not a completion, nor a fulfillment of the thought, but an accentuated restatement, a fervent prayer in and of itself.

Time and distance have deprived us of all the particulars of the satirical piece which is Ballade 91. But here Charles d'Orléans, the "gentle," sophisticated, courtly poet shows himself a witty match for a later rival, Joachim DuBellay. It is of no real consequence to identify the owner of this "Visage de baffe venu / Confit en composte de vin." What is noteworthy for the purposes of this

---

[5] See appendix for complete schema of ballade refrains.

analysis is the syntactical character of the refrain in relation to the message. It adds nothing new but clearly fixes in the reader's mind the emotional tone of the poem: "Dieu le me sauve ce varlet!"

In brief, the common denominator in each of these examples is the way in which the refrain is consciously set apart from the body of the stanza in order to reinforce the principal theme, or more often still, the psychological content. The thrust is outwards and away from the text. The very nature of the syntax thus suggests an audience for whom performance seems the objective.

Far more frequently, however, the typical refrain in the ballades by Charles d'Orléans is grammatically tied to its stanza. One finds three distinct forms of this type of refrain: (1) appositional (2) conjunctional (3) complementary.[6] A few examples will help to ascertain if a different kind of syntactical-thematic relationship occurs in this classification of refrain.

The Appositional Refrain

One can identify at least three ballades (2, 22, 54)[7] which fall into this category. By definition, the appositional form does not complement the grammatical structure of which it is nonetheless a syntactical member. It does not, in other words, complete or add new information. Like the unlinked refrain, it has an essentially tautological function.

In Ballade 2, the refrain is a traditional courtly form of polite address, "Ma seule souveraine joye," directed toward the object of the poet's amorous entreaties. It is no more than a conventional salutation, placed here at the end of the stanza rather than at the beginning, for the purpose of emphasis. In Ballade 22, the refrain, "Dieu scet en quel mauvais party," has no real complementary relationship to what precedes and merely

---

[6] Although, for the sake of clarity and simplification, these grammatical classifications take some liberties, they respect the traditional syntactical analyses of most French grammarians. See for example Maurice Grévisse, *Précis de grammaire française*.

[7] Ballade 86, it should be noted in this regard, is a rather unique case, since it constitutes a "double refrain." But if one views the two final lines as a *single* refrain, two out of the three stanzas are in fact appositional in nature.

stresses the poet's affliction. Similarly, the refrain of Ballade 54, "Ma Dame, ma seule maistresse," is a courtly greeting.

In each of these cases, therefore, the appositional refrain, similar to those which are in fact grammatically unlinked to the stanza, has a purely *reiterative* function.

The Conjunctional Refrain

The whole issue becomes considerably more complex when we appproach the conjunctional refrains. To begin with, these may be grammatically identified as follows:

1. Ainsi que 103
2. Avant que 96
3. Fors que 13
4. Puis que 10,121
5. Car 1,29,52
6. Comme 61,85,110
7. Quant 30,31,38
8. Si 44,67,87,123

In the same way that the appositional refrain is by definition not linked to the syntax of its stanza, the conjunctional refrain is *necessarily* a part of its grammatical structure. There is, however, the less obvious point of whether it stands in a more reiterative or a more complementary relationship. To put it still more precisely, does it add substantively to the emotional or ideological content?

The first stanza of Ballade 28 belongs to a grammatical unit of four lines whose ideological topos is the familiar leitmotif of distance and separation. The persona receives from his "Belle" the "Nef de Bonne Nouvelle," which has come to him from the "port de Desir . . . ou est a present ma maistresse." The final two lines make up a double qualifier in the form of a relative clause joined by the conjunction "et": "Qui est ma doulce souvenance / Et le tresor de ma lyesse." Thus, while the refrain has a complementary and referential tie to the antecedent "maistresse," it seems to function also as a reiterative element of the relative clause to which it is coupled.

In the following stanza a similar phenomenon takes place

when, in a syntactical unit of five lines the refrain is more clearly a parallel reiteration of the complementary phrase to which it is joined:

> Et, pource, lui plaist m'envoyer
> Ceste nef, plaine de Plaisance,
> Pour estoffer la forteresse
> Ou mon cueur garde l'Esperance
> Et le tresor de ma liesse.

Similarly, in the closing stanza, the refrain forms another more reiterative parallel to the preceding verse: "En qui puis mettre ma fiance / Et le tresor de ma liesse."

A like pattern emerges in Ballade 55, most particularly in the first and second stanzas of this poem. But the reiterative quality of the "et"-type refrain is best exemplified in Ballade 101. In each of the three stanzas here, the refrain, consistently part of a two-line epilogue-like syntactical unit, drives home the theme of politico-military victory for the "franc royaume de France":

1. Leur grant orgueil entierement abat,
   Et t'a rendu Guyenne et Normandie.
2. Or a tourné Dieu ton dueil en esbat,
   Et t'a rendu Guyenne et Normandie.
3. De sa verge dieu les pugnist et bat
   Et t'a rendu Guyene et Normandie

In other instances, however, the complementary character of the refrain appears more clearcut. In Ballade 65, for example, famous for its allusion to the good doctor "Nonchaloir," the refrain is a pointedly melancholic contradiction of what precedes. The first stanza concludes:

> Un bon medecin qu'on appelle
> Nonchaloir, que tiens pour amy,
> M'a guery, la sienne mercy,
> Se la playe ne renouvelle.

In the next stanza it is the man of medicine himself who speaks and the antithetical character of the refrain again becomes very evident:

> "Mais que gardes bien ta fourcelle
> Du vent d'Amours qui te fery,

Tu es en bon point jusqu'a cy,
Se la playe ne renouvelle."

Continuing to proffer medical counsel, Nonchaloir's double-edged remarks are heightened still more by the telescoped form of the closing verses in the final stanza. The clear grammatical reduction, in other words, intensifies the antinomical properties of the refrain: "Lors fus nasvré, or t'ay guery, / Se la playe ne renouvelle."

Though it is thus possible to identify reiterative or complementary functions among these conjunctional-type refrains, there are at least as many cases where the distinctions are blurred and less easy to classify. It would seem that certain of these conjunctions lend themselves to either reiterative (*et*) or complementary (*se/si*) functions by dint of their very grammitico-lexicographical identities. But the associations of form and content depend as much upon syntactical structures as they do upon the inherent qualities of the conjunctions themselves and that is a question to which we will have to return. For the moment, however, let us proceed to our final category.

The Complementary Refrain

By far the lion's share of refrains in Charles d'Orléans' ballades fall into this last classification and can be summarized by the following grammatical sub-headings:

1. Relative pronoun 33
2. Subordinate clause 49,82,92,107
3. Infinitive 12,46,67,75,78,109, 122
4. Adverb 3,11,42,48,88
5. Noun 7,16–18,20,34,47,63, 73,77,92,94,102,105
6. Prepositions 5,24,27,32,39,45,57, 66,68,70,79,81,84,95

Obviously the issue here is not *whether* the refrain complements but *how* or, more exactly, *how much*. For even in the case of a complementary function, the refrain will relate to its stanza in some greater or lesser degree of complementarity.

Not surprisingly, for example, when the refrain performs the syntactical operation of dependent clause, the complementarity is at its maximum, since its absence would render the meaning incomplete. Without the refrain, the sentence would make no sense. In Ballade 82, in the first stanza, the refrain is indispensable to the completion of the idea: "Si fais a toutes gens savoir / Qu'encore est vive la souris!" In similar fashion, the refrain to Ballade 107 is essential to the thought. Here is the conclusion to the third stanza: "J'en ay ouy parler assez de tieulx / Qui sont tous sains, quoyque point ne desnye / Que m'aimez bien, et vous encore mieulx."

The same appears to be true of many noun complements. There is no way, for example, of making sense of Ballade 7 without its refrain: "Je vous asseure, par ma foy, / Que je n'en sauroye garder / Mon cueur qui est maistre de moy."

In Ballade 18, the second stanza reads: "Lors trouveray, je ne sçay s'il dit voir, / Le plus grant bien qui me puist avenir." The sentence is again meaningless without the refrain to complete the thought.

In Ballade 37, one discovers the same sort of strong complementarity when "Espoir" addresses the poet's "cueur" thus: "Je vous fais loyalle promesse / Que je vous garde seurement / Tresor d'amoureuse richesse."

There are, however, as many examples in which the refrain retains its complementary character but is not inextricably bound to the meaning. It has, in other words, a clear reiterative relationship to the sentence to which it belongs.

In the second stanza of Ballade 67, the infinitive clause certainly functions as much reiteratively as complementarily: "Il vous convient sien demourer, / Sans departir, jusqu'a la mort."

Likewise, the second stanza of Ballade 78 strengthens the theme without being utterly indispensable to its meaning: ". . . pour ce, soyez soigneuses / De recevoir leur plaisant compaignie/Pour resveillier voz pensees joieuses."

Adverbial complements also have a tendency to be tautological and emphatic rather than crucial to the completion of the meaning:

> Et si me fait demourer en soussy,
> Loings de celle par qui puis recouvrer

Le vray tresor de ma droitte esperance
Et que je vueil obeir et amer
Treshumblement, de toute ma puissance. (42)

The third stanza of Ballade 53 ends thus: "Car Amour, en son abbaye, / Le tenoit chief de son couvent. / Du temps [qu'ay congneu en ma vie.]"

There is only one relative pronoun clause, appearing in the form of a dialogue in Ballade 33, and it too has a very minimal complementary function. In each case, the refrain serves more to emphasize than to add substantively to the significance:

1. C'est de vostre Dame et amye
   Qui loyaument fait son devoir.
2. Amour, humblement j'en mercie
   Qui loyaument fait son devoir
3. Bien doit estre dame chierie,
   Que loyaument fait son devoir.

The prepositional-type refrain offers the largest number of examples in this category, indeed, in any of the categories reviewed thus far, and therefore, deserves special attention.

According to the customary functions of the prepositional complement, these refrains in Charles d'Orléans can be identified as complements of:

1. Place.................. 24,27,32,45,66,95
2. Time................... 53,79,117
3. Manner................. 57,84,99,111,112

A few are more difficult to categorize (39,68,70,119).

In any event, we shall want to examine a few examples to judge the relationship between syntax and theme. There are a certain number of these prepositional refrains in which the degree of complementarity is minimal. Strictly speaking, the metaphoric refrain of Ballade 27: "En la prison de Desplaisance"—complements the sentence to which it is syntactically allied, yet it is never crucial to an understanding of the ideational construct. Ballade 57 offers a parallel example. The refrain, "En paine, sousi et doleur" serves more to emphasize the sentiment already expressed than to complete or explicate it. The refrain to Ballade 66 is once again cleverly turned, but this metaphor too enhances the thematic topos more than it explains it. A characteristic use of this type of refrain is Ballade 68 where it can hardly be considered indispensable to comprehending the poem:

> Belle, se ne m'osez donner
> De voz doulx baisiers amoureux,
> Pour paour de Dangier courroucer,
> Qui tousjours est fel et crueux,
> J'en embleray bien un ou deux;
> Mais que n'y prenez desplaisir
> Et que le vueilliez consentir,
> Maugré Dangier et ses conseulx.

In this instance, indeed, the refrain, despite its complementarity, strikes one as plainly redundant.

A similar kind of construction is to be found in Ballade 112 where the prepositional refrain does little more than reinforce what has already been said:

> Desormais en gouvernement
> Me metz et es mains de Vieillesse,
> Bien sçay qu'y vivray soubrement,
> Sans grant [espargne de liesse.]

A somewhat smaller portion of these refrains, however, does establish strong complementarity and cannot be eliminated without seriously weakening the meaning. A good case in point is Ballade 81 whose opening stanza would be an incomplete idea were it not for the prepositional refrain which both concludes the poetic form and its content:

> Cueur, trop es plain de folie.
> . . . .
> Avecque toy demourrons,
> Car c'est le commandement
> De Fortune, qui en serre
> T'a tenu moult longuement
> Ou royaume d'Angleterre.

Another good example is Ballade 111 in which, without the explicative refrain, one would not understand the psychosomatic nature of these physical disorders:

> Migraine de plaignans ardeurs,
> Transe de sommeil mipartie,

> Fievres frissonnans de maleurs,
> Chault ardant fort en reverie,
> Soif que Confort ne rassasie,
> Dueil baigné en froides sueurs,
> Begayant et changement couleurs
> Par le vent [de Merencolie.]

    On an analagous theme, Ballade 117 also depends heavily upon its refrain in order to make clear that the real issue is aging:

> Escollier de Merencolie,
> A l'estude je suis venu,
> Lettres de mondaine clergie
> Espelant a tout ung festu,
> Et moult fort m'y treuve esperdu.
> Lire n'escripre ne sçay mye
> Dez verges de Soussy batu,
> Es derreniers jours de ma vie.

* * * *

    Two important characteristics should by now have become clear. The refrain can, whatever its specific grammatical ties to the preceding syntax, serve either to complete (complement) the stanza's message or merely to reinforce (reiterate) its meaning. Moreover, a just definition of the refrain in Charles d'Orléans' ballades calls for an examination which goes beyond an analysis of the *kind* of syntactical link (or absence of it). It must also examine its more fundamental relationship to the entire sentence structure. The analysis, in other words, must also take full cognizance of the inner dynamics which make up the syntax. And it is to that question which we must now give our attention. The problem is of course extremely complex and we shall concentrate on the most conspicuous and therefore most accessible examples. In a number of ballades, the sentence structure extends from one end of the stanza to the other.

    The first of these one-sentence verse phenomena is to be found in the last stanza of ballade 10. What purports to be a courtly poem addressed to the longed for absent person, takes on, however, a far broader psychological analysis of self, revealing deeper insecurities. What is clear, in any case, is that those emotions are intricately and inextricably woven into the very fabric of the syntax.

Suddenly a tone of saturnine disillusionment appears to give way to hope. The change is marked by the opening conjunction of opposition "Et non pourtant" and further sustained by a topological expansion of elaborating abstractions: "Doulx confort," "chiere lie," and "joyeux penser." But one is aware of the essentially precarious nature of the temporary euphoria when doubt and fear reemerge: "Vous suppliant que ne vueilliez changier." The alternation continues in another about-face of reassurance and expectation: "Car en vous sont tous mes plaisirs mondains." This fleeting optimism vanishes with the sad reminder "desquelz me fault a present deporter." The gloomy final note is restated in the melancholic refrain, "Puis qu'ainsi est que de vous suy loingtains." Ambivalence and a sense of fragile happiness thus find a collaborative restatement in the syntactical fluctuations themselves, for which the refrain is an epilogue of disconsolation.

The opening stanza of Ballade 12 is in and of itself an echo of this theme: "Puis qu'ainsi est que loingtain de vous suis." The inversion, moreover, effectively draws attention to that important fact. Syntax, in brief, corroborates the textual message.

This new treatment of the leitmotif of distance will also make use of syntax to underscore the anguish of separation. Here willful fragmentation creates a jarring motion, cadenced by introspective asides of apprehension. The "dont Dieu scet s'il m'ennuie" reinforces a mood of repressed melancholy. The inner reverberations of self-doubt are brought out by syntagmatic agitation, as if emotional unconscious pulsations were working their way into the poetic discourse's structure. The following "si" clause is yet another good example of this psychogrammatical phenomenon. The main verb "requier" will receive no complement until two other interruptions slow down the motion, one in the form of a cautious apology, the other, in a tautological apposition. When the long-awaited complement is finally identified as "baisier amoureux" and further qualified as "Venant du cueur et de pensee lie," the protracted lexical voyage concludes in a conjunctional refrain whose theme echoes the dark, brooding tone of the entire stanza: "Pour alegier mes griefs maulx doloreux." Lexeme and syntagm work together to sustain the desired mood.

The first stanza of Ballade 15, represents another variation of this intricate interplay between form and content. In this instance the long sentence structure and the emotional content descrescendo from a high pitch of optimism to a refrain of ironic rage. The first four verses capture the ceremonial effervescence of the popular "mois de mai" topos. Suspicion of what is to come appears, however, in the qualifying "Et que l'en doit laissier Ennuy," suggesting an irreconcilable disparity between what should be and what is. Suspicion becomes fact when the persona distinguishes between unfulfilled desire and cruel reality: "Je me treuve sans recouvrance / Loingtain de Joye conquester." The closing three lines of verse simply accentuate the frustration and anxiety which lay thinly veiled behind an earlier heady expression of joy. The underlying message requires that the reader penetrate the apparent discourse to interpret a signification buried beneath the poem's syntagmatic and textual signs.

The closing verse of Ballade 20 provides another example of how the relationship between the refrain and the general syntactical dynamics of the stanza is inextricably bound up with the psychological matrix which engenders the poetic expression. In this structure, the syntax divides into three distinct units, beginning with the dependant "quant" clause which expresses anxious expectancy. A dramatic *enjambement* at line three introduces the second element in a main clause which replaces the emotion of eager hope with an aura of success and even self-adulation, accentuated in the periphrastic trope, at line six, of "loyal devoir." This syntactical triptych concludes with the prepositional phrase "Maugré Dangier qui...", withholding the true emotional ambivalence until the refrain and its preceding line of verse: "Que sans mort en ce point manoir / Ce n'est que miracle d'Amours." In this manner, the psychological impact of uncertainty is conveyed by inverting the entire sentence structure so that the beginning becomes the end: "Ce n'est que miracle d'Amours..."

The same sort of tension is communicated in Ballade 22 by the use of an opening "Combien que" clause. Addressing the beloved, the persona begins with a sarcastic accusation of her indifference intended, it would seem, to elicit some encouraging response. The inculpation serves instead to prepare the way for a long and rueful recital of past sufferings: "Toutesfois se savoir vous plaît . . ." For four lines one reads how beleagured the persona is by a multitude of "maulx," hinted at but never defined. The emotional climax of this involuted self-pity is an appositional refrain which by content and syntax reinforces the unidentified panoply of ills: "Dieux scet en quel mauvais party." Syntactical postponement and lexematic equivocation function thus as the poetic signs of a trauma acknowledged but buried.

In Ballade 24 one finds a poetico-theological construct in which "Amour" (Good) and "Dangier" (Evil) participate in a subtle but trenchant psychomachean struggle. It is the third stanza of this curious pseudo-religious clash of forces which draws our attention, for here again we have one of those lengthy sentences reaching from one end of the stanza to the other and providing yet another example of intimate collaboration between lexeme and syntagm. "Amour" triumphs in her war with evil, wielding the formidable weapons of charity and compassion. She does so by setting an example and coming to the assistance of one "pouvre soufreteux" who becomes the focus of her interest. The psychological content decisively moves from general to specific, from the larger issue to the concrete example. Moreover, the syntagmatic expansion doubles the ideological one, by ineluctably leading the reader to a refrain which aims to win sympathy for the poet-victim, psychologically entrapped "Ou purgatoire de Tristesse." The design of the sentence thus is itself a clear syntactical reiteration of the psychic confinement which it expresses.

In Ballade 32, the first stanza offers yet another interesting example of the complex interweaving of theme and syntax. In this case it concerns the topos of retreat and withdrawal, so characteristic of the Charles d'Orléans poetic discourse. The poem begins in traditional courtly fashion like a one-sided conversation, addressed to an unnamed woman, reduced, as is frequently the case in courtly ideology, to an uncommunicative, captive listener. "Belle, s'il vous plaist escouter." The persona assures her that her heart is in safe keeping, ". . .enveloppé / En ung cueuvrechief de Plaisance." And as if that assurance is not adequate, he adds: "Et enclos, pour plus grant seurté / Ou coffre de ma souvenance." Desire and fear are together locked into a complex syntactical structure which moves backwards and forwards, refusing, it would seem, to conclude.

These are the pervasive anxieties which forever plague the persona and are here expressed in the lexematic collocation of a protracted sentence whose pleonastic refrain reiterates the idea of emotional regression and withdrawal: "Ou coffre de ma souvenance."

Ballade 60 belongs to the moving series of poems composed on the death of a young wife.[8] The first stanza of this ballade builds upon an introductory "Quant" clause which postpones its object pronoun "Celle" until the opening of the third verse. This pronoun in turn engenders three consecutive, deferring auxiliary phrases such that the major clause arrives only at the penultimate line, a climactic, long-awaited noun complement refrain: "Je dy, en pleurant tendrement: / Ce monde n'est que chose vaine!" In a word, the syntactical dalliance adds to the psychological effect of a closing refrain which movingly expresses the persona's crippling despair.

Ballade 78 constitutes one of a trio (78–80) on the theme of time and aging. Again it is the first verse which serves as an example of the single-sentence stanza. There is a striking difference, however, in authorial point of view. Whereas the persona generally speaks for himself, here he assumes a collective perspective. It is "nostre temps" which has paid its debt to *Jeunesse* and, describing the games and merry-making, everyone's point of view which is represented and not just the persona's alone. The syntax moves lightly and swiftly, accumulating qualifiers, like partners in a dance:

> Venuz sommes en ceste mommerie,
> Belles, bonnes, plaisans et gracieuses,
> Pretz de dancer et faire chiere lie,
> Pour resveillier voz pensees joieuses.

The collective, public self projects thus a quite different image

---

[8] "No definitive identification has ever been made of the woman addressed in the ballads. Charles, who refers to her most frequently as "Ma Dame," leaves few clues concerning her identity. The most credible hypothesis, first advanced by Charles's foremost biographer, Pierre Champion, links the *dame* to the poet's second wife, Bonne d'Armagnac. A series of poems lamenting the death of the lady (a "noble Princesse") appears to coincide with Bonne's death prior to 1436." David Fein, *Charles d'Orléans*, p. 18.

when compared, for example, with the more personal and private melancholy expressed elsewhere. This mask of bright resignation, which the persona will don more readily in later years, is re-echoed in the sprightly sing-song rhythm. And the nearly frantic enthusiasm of text and syntax seems to reach an emotional peak in a refrain whose desperate cry for "pensees joieuses," concludes this symbolic, syntactical dance which is, in fact, the Dance of Death.

Ballade 89 is one of the epistolary poems addressed to the poet's cousin, the Duke of Burgundy. More informational than introspective, the whole poem takes on a kind of reporter's matter-of-fact style and the opening one-sentence stanza shows yet another way in which the content is made to interact with the syntax.

The letter-writer speaks of "Des nouvelles d'Albion," and then continues the statement with a familiar formula phrase: "Si il vous en plaist escouter / Mon frere et mon compaignon." The imperative voice of "Sachez que" underscores the intimacy of the speech, a private exchange, as it were, where we the readers are allowed to listen quietly. There is too a buoyant, zestful character here which is captured by the bouncy, seven-syllable rhythm. The words tumble over each other in a jaunty exuberance which reaches a highpoint of excitement in the refrain's final note of cheerful optimism: "En bons terms ma matiere."

Ballade 98 shows the poet at his most inventive, as he ingeniously transfers mimetic representation to the syntactical dynamics of the poem. In this famous, oft-quoted ballade, Charles describes one of his many trips on the Loire and remarkably captures the motion of the boat in the syntagmatic structure. This gem-like poem intrigues us, moreover, by the fact that the external, mimetic components once again reveal that deeper, psychological reality for which text and syntax are the decodable signs.

Our principal interest lies with the second stanza, but to understand better the emotional context, a word must be said of the preceding verse. Although the opening participial phrase suggests the desired forward motion, the sudden inversion which appears in the next line, simultaneously puts the verb into a focal position and creates an unexpected break in the dynamics: "En tirant d'Orléans a Blois / L'autre jour par eau venoye." The contrast between arrested motion and uninterrupted movement comes from the careful juxtaposition of the final six lines. Like the steady advance of the passing boats, the discourse thereafter progresses "legierement" toward the ballade's refrain. But it is finally with the philosophical statement of the refrain, emphasizing the boat's dependence upon the "plaisir et gré" of the wind, that one comprehends the fundamental pessimism of the poem.

> Si rencontré, par plusieurs foiz
> Vaisseaux, ainsi que je passoye,
> Qui singloient leur droicte voye
> Et aloient leigerement,
> Pour ce qu'eurent, comme veoye,
> A plaisir et a gré le vent.

The metaphoric language as well as the poem's sentence structure conceal a meaning which requires careful decoding of both lexeme and syntagm.

That is yet more evident in the second stanza, another of those uninterrupted syntactical units stretching from start to close of the verse. The point is that if in the first stanza, the refrain is the logical culmination of an observed fact, in the second stanza of the ballade, it becomes more clearly the expression of the persona's anxieties, the fear of unfulfilled expectations. The voyage turns into a psychological excursion, and the persona's fellow passengers become extensions of his inner self: "Mon cueur, Penser et moi." Together they watch, together they hope. But it is finally "cueur," that frightened Other, more frequently scrutinized then scrutinizer, who puts the persona's anxieties into words, and in so doing creates a contrast between the *textual* sign of stagnation and the *syntagmatic* sign of motion:

> Mon cueur, Penser et moy, nous troys,
> Les regardasmes a grant joye
> Et dit mon cueur a basse vois:
> "Voulentiers en ce point feroye,
> De confort la voille tendroye
> Se je cuidoye seurement
> Avoir, ainsi que je vouldroye
> A plaisir et a gré de vent.

The poetic discourse provides thus a revealing glimpse into the invisible reality which Lacan calls the "ailleurs" or "Autre scène."[9]

No doubt the extreme case of the syntactical phenomenon under review is Ballade 111 where all three stanzas constitute examples of unbroken, single sentences. The explanation is quite simple: one is dealing with enumeration, mock enumeration of medical disorders, to be sure, but enumeration, nonetheless. The syntactical device, in brief, is a part of the persona's black humor, in the last analysis perhaps not meant to be amusing at all! In any event, the poet deftly manipulates the technique and proves he is able to put it to many uses.

The final ballade which offers an example of the single-sentence stanza is Ballade 118. It is one of a pair of ballades, back to back, in which the persona speaks of his "Chambre de pensee" establishing immediately a mood of self-analytical introspection. The mimetic representation upon which the descriptive analysis is built is that of a council of war. The lines of battle are defined and defeat seems imminent:

> L'autre jour tenoit son conseil
> En la chambre de ma pensee,
> Mon cueur qui faisoit appareil
> De deffence contre l'armee
> De fortune, mal advisée,
> Qui guerryer vouloit Espoir, . . .

The internal dynamics of the sentence push forward toward the noun subject "mon cueur", reserved to the end of the introductory adverbial qualifier, three lines into the poem. The ungrammaticality makes clear that "cueur" is not only the syntactical center of the stanza but the psychological nucleus. The following relative clause leads to an important qualifier "mal advisée," which draws attention to the essential tone of despair. A second relative clause completes the image of confrontation. But at that crucial juncture, a final "se" clause provides a sudden upward swing in the emotional content, with the key word *Espoir* as the logical and grammatical link between the two opposing sentiments. The prepositional refrain is the final expression of the persona's longing for "Bon Eur

---

[9] Jacques Lacan, *Ecrits*, pp. 548–49.

et Loyal Vouloir." Moreover, that coupling of happiness and the poet's longed-for good wishes of those who must judge him, constitute a central place in the fundamental psychic struggle for which the war allegory in this ballade is a mere poetic substitute or psychological displacement.[10]

* * * *

In sum, the syntactical relationship between refrain and stanza echoes the dialectical reflection / deflection topos of the ballade. On the one hand, there are those refrains which have a clearly tautological function. They repeat or accentuate.[11] They restate the topos in some emphatic fashion and, as such, seem more closely allied to the dance traditions of the form.[12] They pull out and away from the psychic center of the creative impetus, in other words, away from the persona and toward an audience. They therefore appear to be less introspective, less self-revealing, more theatrical and performance-oriented. They are *deflective* in nature, humor and wit and an open light-heartedness often preempting self-analysis and introspection. Such is the case in all the ballade refrains which have no syntactical link at all to their stanza; such too would seem to be the case of the "appositional-type" refrains.[13]

On the other hand, there are those ballade refrains more intimately concerned with self and personal scrutiny than with any sort of audience effect. They are *reflective* in nature. The attention is turned inwards toward the creator. In them, self

---

[10] "The text functions something like a neurosis: as the matrix is repressed, the displacement produces variants all through the text, just as suppressed symptoms break out somewhere else in the body." Richael Riffaterre, *Semiotics of Poetry*, p. 19.

[11] Poirion sees this as the typical thematic function of the ballade refrain in the poetry of Charles d'Orléans: "La répétition du refrain apparaît moins comme la marque de l'action que comme l'écho de l'émotion." *Le Poète et le prince*, p. 394.

[12] "Quoi qu'il en soit, la structure, avec son refrain répété à la fin de chaque strophe, est caractéristique du lyrisme qui dérive de la danse." Poirion, *Le Poète et le prince*, p. 367.

[13] Paul Zumthor interestingly notes on this point: "Le terme de 'refrain' en effet, fréquent dans l'usage médiéval, s'y réfère à la récurrence d'une coupure (*frangere* plus qu'à la répétition de mots, comme nous l'entendons aujourd'hui." *Essai de poétique médiévale* (Paris: Seuil, 1972), p. 246.

speaks to self, creating thus a kind of internal monologue. While the specific grammatical link might be either conjunctional or complementary, in these the refrain gains its significance from the way it expands, clarifies or, in a word, complements text. Furthermore, these refrains are often deeply imbedded in the syntagmatic fabric, on occasion going back to the very beginnings of the stanza. We have counted no less than twenty such examples.

Remembering of course that the bulk of the ballades are of the three-stanza variety, it is also noteworthy that there are well over 80 ballades (65%) in which one can find a refrain sentence-structure of four or more lines of verse, more than 50 (40%) in which this is true of two of the stanzas, and no less than 16 cases (12%) in which it is true of three stanzas of the ballade. There is, in brief, evidence that this syntactical density is not entirely aleatory, but a noteworthy syntactical fact, and as such, an unconscious communication emerging from that "autre scène" whose language requires decoding. And what, in psychological terms does this signify?

Apart, to be sure, from other lexematic considerations, one would be hard pressed to offer a meaningful psychosemiotic reading of such statistics. But coupled with the other indicators, it seems probable that the sentence structure here corroborates the essentially reflective character of the ballade. The syntactical inward thrust parallels the textual signs of introspection.

But what is to be concluded about that apparently opposite tendency to enclose the persona behind the syntactical doors, as it were, of the refrain? Is this to be construed as an antithetical movement, contradicting the other? How does one argue away the seeming inconsistency? Are the deflective and reflective tendencies psychically incompatible?

The explanation is of course quite simple. The two phenomena are in fact double sides of the same psychological reality, to the extent that deflection and reflection are both protective devices. Both point to the same fundamental truth about the persona, vulnerable, anxious, eager to receive approbation, afraid of rejection. That psychic fact is replicated in a syntax which turns inwards and also deflects from the private self.

As for the internal dynamics of the one sentence stanzas,

their syntactical fluctuations suggest a more than accidental correlation with the emotional content of the text. They too are an important part of the unconscious message.[14] They too corroborate the psychic portrait of the persona which emerges from the form and topoi of the ballades.

Before drawing any more general conclusions, however, about the latent language of the poetic discourse, either lexematic or syntactical, there are still crucial questions which need to be answered. To begin with, and above all, will a psychosemiotic reading of the remaining works by Charles continue to substantiate this interpretation of the poetic text? Are the exigetical determinants of deflection and reflection, in brief, adequate for any sort of all-encompassing psychological explanation of the persona's inner life?

We must thus turn to that other vast body of lyrical work, to the nearly 450 rondeaux which, for the most part, were created after Charles d'Orléans' long separation from country, family and friends.

---

[14] Le Galliot identifies the Lacanian methodology in these apt terms: "Le texte n'est donc pas simple jeu réglé des signifiants, ce qui ferait de lui une pure logique algorithmique, se soutenant de sa propre existence et opérant hors toute détermination spatio-temporelle. . . . La vérité du texte est à saisir en un autre lieu. . . . c'est le lieu de la psychanalyse." *Psychanalyse et langages littéraires*, p. 202. It is, interesting, in this regard, to read what Roland Barthes says in his fascinating autobiography about the search for his own "authentic" self. Indeed, the conscious use of the third person pronoun already tells the story: "Son malaise, parfois très vif-allant certains soirs, après avoir écrit toute la journée, jusqu'à une sorte de peur-, venait de ce qu'il avait le sentiment de produire un discours double, dont le mode excédait en quelque sorte la visée." *Roland Barthes par roland barthes* (Paris: Seuil, 1975), pp. 52–3.

Chapter 3
Paradox and Masks

> Qui est descouvert, mal se cache....
> (Rondeau 150)

In the period following his long English imprisonment, the newly-liberated poet projects in the rondeaux, the form which he now appears to prefer,[1] the image of a fun-loving persona in search of distraction and games: "Allons nous esbatre, / Mon cueur, vous et moy...." (52) Here one finds an energetic "moi" who eagerly dons a "joyeuse maniere" (52), coaxes friends into delightful verbal games of wit, and seems, for the first time, to discover the magic of a thriving, colorful world *outside* of himself:

> Tant embasmees sont de odeurs
> Qu'il n'est cueur qui ne rajeunie,
> En regardant [ces belles fleurs.] (34)

And yet, the themes of withdrawal and reflection not only persist but take on increasing prominence in all of this later poetry. More than ever the persona opts for the quiet confidentiality

---

[1] We are accepting Cigado's chronology of composition which places virtually all the rondeaux sometime after the poet-prince's return to France. *L'Opera poetica*.

40

of his "chambre de pensee," more than ever he seeks asylum from a world which might inflict pain (95,110), more than ever he speaks of retreating into his own private sanctum:

> Ne hurtez plus a l'huis de ma Pensee,
> Soing et soussi, sans tant vous traveiller,
> Car elle dort et ne veult s'esveiller, (298)

One has already seen in the ballade the paradox of a reflective persona who also distances or deflects himself from inner anguish through the creation of a second self which he names "cueur." Here rather, the deflective technique appears in the form of masking. The persona protects the sensitive, private "moi" by assuming various psychological postures. He deals with the basic conflict between public and private self by hiding the latter behind the former. That masking is communicated directly and indirectly in both lexematic and syntagmatic signs of the poetic discourse. Let us look first at the content before turning to the form of the rondeau.

A. Plaisance

Released from political custody, the anguished "moi" is by no means freed from his chronic psychological imprisonment. In the background remains the haunting, persistent image of "douloureuse Merancolie." (396)[2] The passage of time, moreover, seems only to have increased his vulnerability. If only he could, he would most certainly banish despair and gloom forever:

> Qui est celluy qui s'en tendroit
> De bouter hors Merencolie,
> Quant toute chose reverdie,
> Parles champs, devant ses yeulz, voit?
> . . . .
> Par raison, chascun le devroit. (258)

The key word is of course "raison," since the unhappy persona

---

[2] See the perceptive, semiotic analysis of this topos in Jean Starobinsky, "L'Encre de la mélancolie." Nouvelle Revue française 123 (1963): 410–423.

realizes all too well that there can be no escape from that which is *beyond* reason:

> [C]'est la prison Dedalus
> Que de ma merencollie,
> Quant je la cuide fallie,
> G'i rentre de plus en plus. (411)

He is trapped, as trapped as ever he was in England, except that *this* imprisonment offers no hope for escape. There can only be the fleeting, temporary escape born of distractions, all of which gives to the persona's frantic search for amusement a frightening, existential quality of pascalian anguish. And thus it is that the pursued becomes the pursuer, the jailed the jailor: "S'en mez mains une foix vous tiens / Pas ne m'eschaperez Plaisance." (45)

Critics have written much about the topos of confinement in the poetry of Charles d'Orléans, but they have not always seen the ambiguities of its psychological implications.[3] The traumatized "moi" must separate himself as much from old hurts as potential new ones. Paradoxically therefore, he fears the imprisonment which is the inescapable reality of his psychological self, at the same time that he seeks to enclose himself in an artificial atmosphere of protection from possible pain. In that sense thus, the mask of *plaisance* is one form of creating protective confinement. He hides his hurts not only from an intruding world of observers but also from himself;

> Plus penser que dire
> Me couvient souvent,
> Sans moustrer comment
> N'a quoy mon cueur tire.
> Faignant de sousrire
> Quant suis tresdolent,
> Plus [penser que dire
> Me couvient souvent.] (46)

---

[3] The general assumption is that the withdrawal into self represents retreat into a safe harbor, away from danger in the hostile *outside* world: "Le corps est le château de l'âme, dont il faut surveiller et au besoin colmater les percées, les portes." Planche, *Charles d'Orléans ou la recherche d'un langage*, p. 246. "L'âme s'enferme dans le corps pour échapper aux assauts du monde extérieur." Poirion, *Le Poète et le prince*, p. 570.

The mimetic signifier of that enclosure which keeps out the enemy "merancolie," is of course the resident castle at Blois. But it is in turn signified by the fantasy world of *plaisance* which Charles creates within its decor, where he plays courtly poet, courtly lover, and courtly host. There he welcomes pleasure and banishes despair. (43) There he forgets old sorrows and envisages a happy flight beyond the clutches of "Dangier," "Soussi," and "Ennui:"

> Quant commanceray a voler
> Et sur elles me sentiray,
> En si grant aise je seray. (72)[4]

There, in a word, he puts on the mask of *Plaisance* because he so fears the alternative:

> J'iray tout bellement
> Pour paour de me lasser
> Et sans trop m'en lasser
> Ou monde follement,
> Tellement [quellement] (157)

The poet thus seeks to protect self from self, for the incarceration of the deeper "moi," haunted by the recollection of past sufferings as well as by fears of new personal disappointments, is more cruel than any he has tasted in either military or political confrontation, more nagging and abiding,—like some chronic ailment:

> [J]e suis a cela
> Que Merancolie
> Me gouvernera. (376)

And that immovable, unrelenting psychic malaise he covers over with the "Mommerie" of empty words and gestures:

> Pour mieulx embler priveement Plaisance,
> Mommerie, sans Parler de la bouche,
> En beaux abiz d'or cliquant d'Acointance,
> Soubz visieres de Semblant qu'on my touche. (121)

---

[4] The symbol of flying in traditional Freudian analysis has always had sexual significance. *The Interpretation of Dreams*, translated by A. A. Brill (New York: Macmillan, 1913), p. 239. By extension, however, one could relate it to the desire to escape, the desire to fulfill the fundamental wish of freedom from anxiety.

It is a philosophical choice, a very conscious *masking* technique, a willful psychological artifice meant to shut out the truth:

> Il ne me chault ne de chien ne d'oyseau
> Quant tout est fait, il fault passer sa vie
> Le plus aise qu'on peut, en chiere lie.
> A mon advis, c'est mestier bon et beau,
> [Souper ou baing et disner ou bateau.] (347)

The beleaguered "moi" indulges thus in the most cynical kind of hedonism. He has confronted the drama of solitude and self-reflection and has wittingly fled from them in favor of the blissful forgetfulness which comes of laughter and an invented world of chimeric pleasures:

> [M]ais s'entour moy pluseurs de voy,
> Et qu'on rit, parle, chante ou crye,
> Je chasse hors Merencolye
> (Que tant hayr et craindre doy)
> Quant[me treuve seul, a par moy!] (395)

But he is by no means duped. He realizes all too well that beneath the mask persists the unflagging distress:

> Je vous sans et congnois venir,
> Anuyeuze Merencolie;
> Maintes fois, quant je ne vueil mye,
> L'uys de mon cueur vous fault ovrir. (424)

It is quite simply that he prefers to count himself among the dupers rather than the duped:

> A trompeur trompeur et demi;
> Tel qu'on seme couvient cuillir;
> Se mestier voy partout courir,
> Chascun y joue et moy aussi. (163)

B. Le Monde Vivant

In the conventional courtly idiom, the eyes transmit the vision of hoped for pleasure: "Les yeulz si sont fais pour servir, / Et pour raporter tout plaisir." (C 53) as well as the threat of potential danger: "Car plus voys ou monde vivant / Et mains me plaist, ainsi m'aist Dieux." (92)[5] Although this ambivalence is in itself another important textual key to interpreting the persona's psyche, there remains the incontestable fact that the later poetry manifests an increasing awareness of the *monde vivant*.[6] This crucial change is integrally bound up with the larger issue of an evolving metaphysical vision which slowly turns allegory into symbol and symbol into textual sign.[7] The result is a conscious objectivization in which mimetic representation assumes a new valorization for its own sake without, however, losing its value as a psychological sign.[8] Quite to the contrary, for at the same time that this mimetic process endows the sign with a new authenticity, it also functions as part of the persona's deflecting technique. It is, in fact, another kind of masking, one which deliberately turns the poetic vision away from the self and out toward a newly discovered world of describable objects. The explanation of this apparent paradox is more apparent when one accepts the fundamental premise that *d*eflection is always *r*eflection because *every* sign offers the opportunity to uncover the unconscious self. To this question we shall return later; suffice it to say here that Charles seems suddenly to take much greater account of the world around him.

To be sure, the persona continues to speak in terms of "La forest de Longue Actente (228) and "L'eau de Pleur, de Joy ou de Douleur / Qui fait moudre le molin de Pensee." (285). The object

---

[5] Traditional readings of the text, however, generally refuse to go beyond the more obvious courtly interpretations of these allusions. In a psychosemiotic approach, the eyes and what they see take on of course, a much broader signification.

[6] "The later poet drew more and more upon his eyes, which seemed to have been opened for the first time around 1440." Goodrich, *Charles of Orleans*, p. 130.

[7] "La pratique sémiotique du signe assimile ainsi la démarche métaphysique du symbole et la projette sur 'l'immédiatement perceptible;' ainsi valorisé, 'l'immédiatement perceptible' se transforme en *objectivité* qui sera la loi maîtresse du discours de la civilisation du signe." Julie Kristeva, *Sémeiotiké: Recherches pour une sémioanalyse* (Paris: Seuil, 1960), p. 118.

[8] "La Métaphore se charge de saveur, de poids: elle redevient réalité aussi authentique que l'autre, plus authentique même." Paul Zumthor, "Charles d'Orléans et le langage de l'allégorie," in *Mélanges offerts à Rita Lejeune*, 2 vols., (Gembloux: J. Duculot, 1969) II:1501.

is still inextricably attached to its non-objective signification, in the metaphoric manner customary in nearly all of this poetry. In the rondeaux, however, one discovers more and more examples in which the descriptive elaboration goes beyond the use of the object as symbol, to constitute an intermediary stage between "pure" description and allegory.

There are, for example, the protracted voyage metaphors of Rondeaux 333 and 433, to say nothing of a particularly comic expansion on the topos of "l'Amoureuse cuisine" in Rondeau 283:

> Il souffist de tendre geline
> Qui soit sans octz, ne veilles peaux
> Mainssee de plaisans cousteaux;
> C'est au cueur vraye medecine,
> Dedans [l'amoureuse cuisine.]

Developing the well-known spring topos of the troubadours, the poet offers this picturesque passage:

> Lez oyseaus deviennent danseurs
> Dessuz mainte branche flourie
> Et font joyeuse chanterie,
> De contres, deschans et teneurs,
> En regardant [ces belles fleurs.] (34)

But there are also those instances in which objectivization serves no apparent purpose beyond the description itself. Everyone is of course abundantly familiar with the much-quoted nature poems of Charles d'Orléans announcing the arrival of warmer days (30) and the departure of winter (31):

> Mais vous, Yver, trop estes plain
> De nege, vent, ploye et grezil;
> On vous deust banir en essil. (333)

Moreover, he does not limit himself to meteorological phenomena. There is, for example, this touching homage to his dog:

> A toute heure diligemment traveilles,
> Et en chasse vaulz autant qu'un limier,
> Tu amaines, au tiltre de levrier,
> Toutez bestes, et noires et vermeilles:
> Pres la [briquet aus pendantes oreilles!] (167)

Often enough also the mimetic process becomes a way of memorializing events of no great significance:

> Aux champs, par hayes et buissons,
> Perdriz et lyevres nous prendrons,
> Et yrons pescher sur rivieres,
> Puis que par deça [demourons,
> Nous, Saulongnois et Beausserons,
> En la maison de Savonnieres.] (338)

However, in any psychosemiotic analysis of text, a strict dichotomization of symbol/object must by definition be viewed as essentially arbitrary, for every poetic sign is in fact part of the decodable system. And in the psychological context of which we are speaking, this objectivization functions as an important part of the persona's tactic of deflection. The entire mimetic process can be interpreted as a psychological device which turns the persona's vision away from present deceptions and the painful recollection of past hurts.

Much of course has been said about the role of nature in lyric poetry. It is interesting in this regard to point out, however, that whether descriptions of the *monde visible* appear to be a deflective process, as they most probably are here, or part of a consciously reflective process, as they most certainly are in later Romantic verse, in either case, the text leads back to the *un*conscious persona, back ultimately to that *Autre* who inevitably intrudes upon the discursive self.[9] And in this instance at least, the message unmistakably substantiates the general psychological analysis. It speaks in the language of a wounded "moi" seeking protection and relief.

C. Nonchaloir

Critical readings of the Charles d'Orléans' text commonly emphasize the topos of withdrawal as expressed in the signifier

---

[9] "L'inconscient, à partir de Freud, est une chaîne de signifiants qui quelque part (sur une autre scène, écrit-il) se répète et insiste pour interférer dans les coupures qui lui offre le discours effectif et la cogitation qu'il informe." Lacan, *Ecrits*, p. 799.

Nonchaloir.[10] But explanations have often tended to be somewhat too categorical and simplistic as we have had occasion to point out already.

The persona continues to speak of the asylum of his inner self:

> Quelque chose derriere
> Couvient tousjours garder,
> On ne peut pas monstrer
> Sa voulenté entiere. (67)

His privacy is his treasure (324) where he hopes to store up "Joyeuse Promesse" in a "coffin d'Oublie." (428), because the earlier anxieties about a hostile world outside himself persist. But an important new element has been added to this psychological drama, and that new element is advancing old age. Increasingly linked to the topos of *Nonchaloir* now, is that of *Vieillesse*, which seems to provide a convenient shield against the temptations of indulging too much his love for distraction. This is the antithesis of the same deflecting tactic. It is the answer to the voices of doubt and suspicion, uncertainty and anxiety. There is thus in these later poems, a semblance of stoic resignation, even a near-fatalistic acquiescence to things as they are. In some instances the persona turns into a disciple of Marcus Aurelius, or, more likely still, Boethius:[11]

> Viengne que advenir pourra!
> Chascun a sa destinee,
> Soit que desplaise, ou agree;... (68)

This new persona speaks of quiet acceptance:

> A quiconque plaise ou desplaise,
> Quant Vieillesse vient les gens prendre,

---

[10] "Two themes dominate his whole work. Love reigns over the first half, while 'nonchalance' permeates the poems of his maturity. All the other themes, whether of nature, fortune or peace, are quite secondary." Harold Watson, "Charles d'Orléans: 1394–1465," *Romanic Review* 61 (February: 1965): 4.

[11] "In the course of the poet's studies, he fixed upon his prime masters, Boethius, Chaucer, and Lorris, and through them upon such distant ones as Plato, Vergil, Ovid and Cicero." Goodrich, *Charles of Orleans*, p. 210.

> Il couvient a elle se rendre
> Et endurer tout son malaise. (114)

He speaks in tones of a pundit of the submission which comes of experience:

> On aprent a taire et a veoir,
> Selon les temps et les saisons
> Sauves [toutes bonnes raisons.] (149)
>
> Regarde et oy,
> Va peu parlant;
> Dieu tout puissant
> Fera de soy.
> Pense [de toy.] (151)

At times, the resignation takes on a religious quality: "[N']est ce raison que le seigneur / Ait tout a son commandement! (221)"

These, however, are the mere trappings of philosophical discourse.[12] It does not require much textual probing to discover that the pretense of "sagesse" is born less of genuine, unresisting acquiescence than of emotional uncertainty. *Nonchaloir* is by no means a Buddha-like serenity in the face of destiny:

> Serviteur plus de vous, Merancolie,
> Je ne seray, car trop fort y traveille;
> Raison le veult, et ainsi me conseille
> Que le face, pour l'aise de ma vie. (270)

Behind the mask of resigned tranquility appear the signs of bitterness against Time and Fortune. The seeming acceptance of his own decline bears the mark of acrimonious resentment. In half-serious tones he describes himself: "comme un chat, suis viel et chenu." (66) Moreover, many are the sardonic references to a young generation of "gorgias" whose presence reminds the persona of his own physical and moral diminution:

> Ilz portent petiz soulers gras,

---

[12] "In spite of the sober connotations attached to certain words normally reserved for a sacred context, these same terms when appearing in Charles's rondeaux often seem to express more whimsy and wit than solemnity of thought." Fein, *Charles d'Orléans*, p. 134.

> A une poulaine embourree;
> Froidure fera son entree
> Par leurs talons nuz par embas:
> Laissez aler [ces gorgias!] (8)

Furthermore the attack is not merely against the demeanor and attire of these young lovers. The jealous anger goes much deeper:

> Que voulez vous que plus vous die,
> Jeunes assotez amourex?
> Par Dieu, j'ay esté l'un de ceulx
> Qui ont eu vostre maladie!
> . . . .
> Mais au derrain, Merencolie
> De ces huis fait passer les ceulx
> En dueil et soussi, Dieu scet quieulx!
> Lors ne chault de mort ou de vie. (60)

This despair goes to the very core of his psychic reality. He may take momentary comfort in some imprecise and abstract concept of ultimate justice: "Chascun son paiement aura..." (63), and like his contemporary Villon, he may even draw some sustenance from the thought of the leveling effects of Death: "Qu'au derrenier, jennes ou vieulx / Mourront tous, par leur grant vaillance. (85)[13]

But nothing will wipe away the pains of former hurts and disappointments; nothing will completely efface the realities of earlier psychic traumas. Wisdom borne of *Vieillesse*, the mask of *Nonchaloir* does not in fact hide the ugly truth which lies buried in the unconscious. All the old pains remain intact, inexorably there to alert the persona to his inescapable vulnerability:

> Vous vistes que je veoye
> Ce que je ne vueil descouvrir,
> Et cognustes, a l'ueil ouvrir,
> Plus avant que je ne vouloye. (145)

Philosophical resignation is tinged inevitably with bittersweet undertones. Acceptance does not come easily. The fragile persona

---

[13] Although the textual signs emerge out of the traditional courtly idiom of love, we are, as ever, more interested in the broader, psychological signification of the poetic discourse here.

wears the mask because its deflective function separates the despairing "moi" from its own enclosure of distress. The persona, at least that part which remains submerged under layers of protective devices, takes ephemeral comfort in a sententious tone which only superficially hides the truth. The enveloping masks, the psychological shields, are an illusion, necessary to survival. They appear to guard a wounded ego from external trauma while they in fact protect self from self. Thus the enclosure topos corresponds emblematically to the apparent antithesis of deflection and reflection. It is a poetic sign which derives from and participates in the fundamental theme of a struggling persona torn between public reality and authentic identity of the inner "moi."

In one sense, *Vieillesse* brings liberation: "Bien sanglé fus d'une estrete couroye / Que, par Age, convient que la deslie: (435), but in another, it can only mean further deprivation and imprisonment: "Temps et temps m'ont emblé Jennesse, / Et laisse es mains de Vieillesse. (420) Old age brings with it, to be sure, a certain wisdom, but, an unsettling one:

> Plus quant qu'on y estudie
> Et mains y congnoit on seurté
> Car de faire de mal bonté
> L'un a l'autre est trop contrarie
> Il faudroit [faire l'arquemie.] (173)

It is a wisdom which recognizes the stubborn persistence of evil, of falsity, of disloyalty, a world of masked manners and bogus smiles. It is in chimera and invention that the restless psyche finds a semblance of rest. It is in fabrication and deception that one pretends to escape. It is in the supposed wisdom of stoic resignation that the truth is buried deep enough so that it hurts less because it is seen less.

And it is this very ambivalence which underscores the persona's relentless and fundamental anguish:

> C'est grant paine que de vivre en ce monde,
> Encore esse plus paine de mourir;
> Si convient il, en vivant, mal souffrir,
> Et au derrain, de mort passer la bonde. (154)

In the end, this quasi-philosophical discourse is yet another poetic device which provides the persona with the shielding mask of resignation (*Nonchaloir*) engendered by the wisdom of advancing years (*Vieillesse*),[14] a very fragile subterfuge at best, one which merely reminds the poet-analyst that enclosure means as much pain as it does comfort and blessed escape. To that paradox, as it relates to the entire psychic drama of the persona, we will need to return shortly. In the meantime, there is still another mask, the most subtle, the most efficacious perhaps, certainly the one which should bring this psychotextual examination of deflection and reflection in the rondeaux of Charles d'Orléans to its logical close.

D. Escrire

The ultimate sign of deflection, the ultimate technique for masking must be the creative act itself.[15] It is *écriture* which provides the pained persona with his most efficacious form of self-evasion, an escape which inevitably retains and explains the "moi" while it attempts not to: "Et mainte chose fiz escrire / En mon cueur, pour le faire rire." (304)

In the rondeaux, more than ever before, the poetic vision takes on a carefree playfulness, a vigorous inventiveness, a verbal cavorting which metamorphoses the creative experience into a pyrotechnical game of language.[16]

---

[14] Planche, however, refuses to acknowledge the psychological signification of *Vieillesse:* "Vieillesse . . . est un signifié et non un signifiant." *Charles d'Orléans ou à la recherche d'un langage,* p. 611.

[15] "Le plus simple, le divertissement, est l'écriture elle'même." Planche,*Charles d'Orléans ou à la recherche d'un langage,* p. 611.

[16] It is well documented that verse competitions, in the manner of the medieval *puys,* were a favorite sport in sophisticated courts like the one at Blois, where more credit was given to wit and skill than to genuine, poetic talent. (Poirion, *Le Poète et le prince,* pp.38-43; 185-89) Charles d'Orléans' personal albums of poetry give ample evidence of these pleasant, literary court activities. The poetic entrees, moreover, are signed, much the same way one would today sign a guest book with some appropriate message. And many of these are identified as the contributions of "Monseigneur d'Orlians," "le duc d'Orlians," "Monseigneur," or quite simply, "Orlians."Three types of poetic games are recognizable. There are those poems which have a common refrain (R. 14, 18, 98, 128, 140, 210-11, 217, 397, 422), those with a common theme (R. 12, 100, 103, 361, 383), and finally those which function like a poetic exchange (R. 1, 19, 21, 101, 156, 358, 364).

At its highest intellectual aspiration, the deflecting humor resides in the clever hyperbolization and witty distortion of metaphor.[17] Language is rendered new by the allegorical vision, as the perceptive and perceiving "yeulx" glean inspiration from an expanding range of human activities: the language of finance (80,88,123–4), medicine (118–119), hunting (C 75), military strategy (C 76), and games (79). Nothing seems sacred, nor beyond recreation, neither religious expression (361) nor even the recollection of personal anguish (383). All is grist for the mill of linguistic sport.

On occasion the comic distortions assume a markedly gallic character:

> Maistre Estienne Le Gout, nominatif,
> Nouvellement, par maniere optative,
> Si a voulu faire copulative;
> Mais failli a en son cas genitif. (19)

The penchant for scatological humor gives the lie to facile, critical dichotomies of criticism which oppose courtly expression to the so-called bourgeois tendencies in literary language.[18] The persona here enjoys the kind of "low-brow" humor more generally associated with the novella and farce:

> Tresfort vous avez combatu,
> Et j'ay mon billart bien tenu;
> C'est beau debat que de deux bons:
> Bien assailly [bien deffendu.] (15)[19]

But at another level, there are more astute turns of phrase, clever plays on words:

> Allez, allez vielle nourice
> De Courroux et de Malle Vie,
> Rassoutée mere Ancolye,
> Vous n'avez que deul et malice. (195)

---

[17] See Riffaterre, *Semiotics of Poetry*, pp. 125–138, for a useful analysis of "Humor as Continuous Catachresis."

[18] Cigado notes that the poet's "umorismo anti-eroica e anti-cortese..." indeed links some of Charles' poetry to works like the *Quinze Joyes de mariage*. *L'Opera poetico*, p. 184.

[19] See also 160 and 172.

One finds whimsical compilations of grammatical constructions such as this comic, rapid-fire sequence of adverbs:

> Plus de desplaisir que de joye,
> Assez d'ennuy, souvent a tort,
> Beaucoup de soucry sans confort,
> Oultraige de peine, ou que soye! (263)

To these are added the half-serious uses of popular aphorisms, still another indication that this poet is not entirely removed from the poetic expressions of that "bourgeois" milieu, that other world of ideas and language. On occasion sentiousness is reduced to the refrain line:

> De legier pleurs a qui la lippe pent. (42)
> Le fer est chault, il le fault batre. (101)
> Chose qui plaist est a demi vendue (123)
> L'aabit le moyne ne fait pas. (126)

But at his most entertaining and playful, the persona offers a rich panoply, an overflowing cornucopia of proverbs, like so many verbal fireworks, tumbling and rising, communicating and obfuscating at the same time:

> Comme j'oy que chascun devise:
> On n'est pas tousjours a sa guise;
> Beau chanter si ennuye bien;
> Jeu qui trop dure ne vault rien;
> Tant va le pot a l'eaue qui brise. (58)

Lexematic deflection slowly gains in prominence, as signifier supercedes signified. Communication at the most rudimentary level is subordinated to the preeminence of verbal creativity. The tendency is manifested finally in the macaronic verse where word play and breaking down of old rules of language for new ones better suits the poetic fancy. It is, in brief, *écriture* as mask:

> *Ubi supra*
> N'en parlons plus
> Des tours cornulz
> *Et cetera* (165)

Paradoxically, speech is intended to deflect meaning as sense borders here on nonsense. *Ubi supra*, the persona writes, let there be no signification, only *et cetera*, that is, the mere semblance of language.

But of course, once again, the technique of depriving speech of connotation removes one layer of communication only to make way for another and the garbled language tells us something in spite of its purported purposelessness.

It may signify the all-too-familiar uncertainty of an anxious "moi:"

> Et vous fault *regere*
> En craintes et rigueurs
> *Noli me tangere*
> Faulte de serviteurs (385) [20]

It may speak of enemies, "trompeurs . . . *non semel sed bis.*" (171) But essentially it is liberation from constraint and a masking of one established set of symbols which enlarge the poetic vision, or more precisely, clarify it. *Poly*language becomes *proto*language. Seeming obscurity and obfuscation in order to turn poetic creation into a reality for its own sake. It is thus illumination through deflection, for behind the verbiage one hears the voice of a desperate "moi" who seeks liberation from self-imprisonment and emblemizes that psychic fact in macaronic mystification and willful distortion or ungrammaticalities. It is the poetic reenactment, in Freudian terms, of destroying communication (the father) in order to create it (the self).[21] The final expression of this phenomenon is the process by which the signifier strives to change places with the signified. At its least obfuscating, it is no more than an amusing amalgam of rhymes:

> Foleurs a fait grandes passees
> Mains cueurs ont tout oultre passé
> Pour ce, par nous soit compassé
> D'eschever faultes compassees,
> Tant que Pasques [soient passees.] (303)

---

[20] See also 166, 169, 256, 327, C 86-7.
[21] See J. Le Galliot, *Psychanalyse et langages littéraires* (Paris: Fernand Nathan,1977), pp. 45–55.

At this semantic level, meaning is subordinated to a preoccupation with homophonic sounds and the gratification which comes with playing rhyme games. Signification, we note, is not absent, merely rendered secondary.

On occasion, the homophonic principle permeates the entire verse line:

> Tellement quellement
> Me faut le temps passer,
> Et soucy amasser
> Maintesfoiz, mallement (157)

> Ci pris, ci mis,
> Trop fort me lie
> Merencolie,
> De pis en pis. (181)

But the persona is quite capable too of carrying the designifying technique farther, when, for example, he introduces nonsense syllables of the child's language:

> Mieulx amassent a gogo
> Gesir sur molz coissinés,
> Car il sont tant poupinés
> Helas! che gnogno, gnogno
> Quant [n'ont assez fait dodo.] (170)

At its most hermetically successful, it is word reduction which whimsically engenders a music-like prattle. Indeed, it is not difficult to imagine these laconic pieces in their song settings:

> Fies vous y!
>   A qui?
>   En quoy
> Comme je voy,
> Riens n'est sans sy.

> Ce monde cy
>   A sy
>   Pou foy.
> Fiés [vous y!]

> Plus je n'en dy,
>   N'escry,

> Pour quoy?
> Chascun j'en croy
> S'il est ainsy;
> Fiés [vous y!] (41)

The evident point is that the conscious search for meaninglessness conveys an unconscious meaning. Poetic deflection is the signifier for a psychic message. Moreover, the poetic discourse here never renounces altogether the desire to disclose and signify. It merely chooses to hint at a translatable value by situating itself halfway between unobscured language and the absence of intelligibility.[22] The deflection, in other words, points to a psychological truth about a persona, torn between the need for self-revelation and the pain which it might provoke, torn between seeking recognition and denying it, torn finally between the private and public person:

> Pense de toy
> Dorenavant,
> Du demourant
> Ie chaille pou. (151)

> Et de cela, quoy?
> En ce temps nouveau,
> Soit ou laid, ou beau,
> Il m'en chault bien poy. (183)

It is as if the persona wants to say more than he dares. The fragmentary, clipped, unfinished phrases which imply more than they state explicitly, represent in fact the psychic unrest underlying them.[23] The enduring paradox, in brief, is that deflection is always

---

[22] "Nonsense is its own sign because it adds a dimension to retroactive reading. Not only does the reader become capable of a structural reading, he becomes sensitized to the semiotic constants pointing to connotations rather than to denotations:..." See Riffaterre, *Semiotics of Poetry*, p. 139. For another perceptive treatment of nonsense as a signifier, see Jean Paris, "The Mortal Sign: Psychological Implications of Linguistic Elements in Literature," in *Literary Criticism and Psychology*, edited by Joseph P. Strelka, pp. 182–86.

[23] "Cette concision est aussi une habileté: elle permet d'être à la fois secret et profond.... Le rondeau se déchiffre comme un visage et non comme un discours." Poirion, *Le poète et le prince*, p. 359.

in the end reflection, when one recognizes that the text is a polygenetic sign with more than one signification.

* * * *

In the ballades, the injured persona seeks refuge in the private recesses of the self. Withdrawal and reflection, however, bring with them painful confrontation with former hurts, so that the reflective "moi" must create psychological distance from himself. In poetic terms that distance comes about through the abstraction of another self which bears the ambiguous cognomen of "cueur." Here in the rondeaux a different set of deflecting devices come into play.

An ever-fragile, traumatized self assumes the beguiling posture of court jester and wit, the fun-loving air of a perceptive observer of people and events, the stoic demeanor of a philosophical sage happily dispensing consoling aphorisms. He turns the poetic discourse itself into a deflecting mask, fashioned from a lexical wizzardry in which signifier and signification often seem to fuse imperceptibly into one.

But however much he hopes to hide within his "sac de joyeuse Promesse," however much he runs from "Anuyeuze Merencolie," his deflective tactics cannot protect him from the haunting image of the "trespiteuse dance" of *Souccy, Vieillesse et Desplaisance*. At best, all he can hope for is the restless sleep of forgetfulness:

>[P]uis chantoient chançons de Pleur,
>Sans musicque, ne accordance;
>D'ennuy, comme ravy en trance,
>M'andormy lors, pour le meilleur,
>Dedens la maison [de Doleur.] (422)

In rondeaux and ballade alike, therefore, the dialectic of deflection/reflection continues to reveal the same psychological phenomenon, the need to withdraw from others and also from the inner "moi." The mask, in other words, serves to deceive both *Other* and *Self*. It remains to be seen finally whether the structural dynamics in the rondeaux duplicate this paradoxical psychic reality.

Chapter 4
The Closed Circle

Mais quant a moy, je m'enfuy.

(R 427)

In the analysis of the ballade refrain we differentiated between two fundamental characteristics in the structural dynamics of the ballade form as used by Charles d'Orléans, and arrived at significant conclusions about the relationship of that form to the conscious and the unconscious content of the poetic discourse. The present review will apply the same methodological principles of analysis to the refrain of the rondeau.[1]

A preliminary word is in order, however, about the special features of the refrain in this so-called fixed form.[2] The crucial fact that the refrain begins the poem, for example, already alters appreciably the manner in which it relates to its stanza. On occasion too the refrain does not appear at all in the middle

---

[1] For a general statistical breakdown of the rondeau refrain see the appendix.
[2] Most recently, Omer Jodogne notes: "C'est à peine si on pourrait encore qualifier le rondeau un poème à forme fixe." "Le Rondeau du XVe siècle mal compris. Du dit et de l'écrit," in *Mélanges de langue et de littérature médiévales offerts à Pierre Le Gentil* (Paris: S.E.D.E.S, 1973), p. 401. See also Poirion, *Le Poète et le prince*, chapitre VIII.

stanza(s).[3] And finally, the typically terse quality of the form, a characteristic upon which Charles d'Orléans capitalizes, changes the perspective of the entire discussion. Nonetheless, as in the case of the ballade refrain, it is possible to make some general statistical remarks, and that no doubt is where our analysis must begin before entertaining any psychological hypotheses about the syntactical dynamics of the rondeau.

The first important quantitative observation concerns the number of verse lines themselves. Charles d'Orléans increasingly chose the double rather than the single line refrain and, on some occasions, even composed rondeaux with three line refrains.[4] Better than 65% of the poems follow this pattern of two or more refrain lines. Less than 35% are of the one line variety. In a tightly woven poetic structure such as the rondeau, this numerical fact is of no small consequence, because it suggests a marked tendency to pull the circle closer together, a *syntactical* fact which underscores a basic *psychological* reality concerning the poetic persona. To this key characteristic we shall return after a structural review of the Charles d'Orléans rondeau.

As we have already learned from the structural analysis of the ballade, there is also the quantitative problem of the syntactical versus the non-syntactical refrain. Taking into account the differences in form, the same principles of definition can, however, apply here. And the statistical evidence is not without interest. One notes that more than 50% of the poems have two out of three stanzas with non-syntactical refrains, refrains which separate themselves from the general syntax of the stanza by their own grammatical structure.

In summary, it should already be clear that Charles d'Orléans takes advantage of the inherent circularity in the rondeau. But how must one interpret these syntactical statistics? On the assumption that form and textual signs are inextricably bound together in any psychosemiotic reading, what do these characteristics reveal? Do

---

[3] 71, 73, 112, 114, 118, 121, 135, 176.
[4] See appendix for complete list.

they corroborate the thematic analysis of the rondeau? Are they consistent with what has been discovered about the persona in the ballade?

The immediate evidence of a conscious structural division of "outer" and "inner" circles seems to argue for an interpretation which describes an anguished "moi" torn between his public and private self. Once again the form would seem to corroborate the principal dialectical topos of reflection/deflection. A closer look at a few examples will help to understand how this takes shape in the rondeau of Charles d'Orléans and whether the facts indeed substantiate the psychological syndrome already delineated.

A. The Hidden Self

Rondeau 12 begins with a blunt, one sentence generalization about human sorrow: "Chascune vielle son dueil plaint." Proffered like some sort of established, indisputable fact about people in general, it is followed by an equally categoric corollary: "Vous cuidez que mal passe / Tout aultre." The uncompromising nature of these parallel statements is reinforced by the abrupt break in the verse line at that point. Then, as if these axiomatic truths come into confrontation with more specific personal judgments, the "moi" intervenes to say, by way of an attenuating corrective: "... mais ja ne parlasse / Du mien, se n'y feusse contraint." The familiar theme of conflict between public and private self is thus expressed in the key words "vielle" and "contraint" which contrast public and individual desires. The ideological disagreement finds a syntactical echo in the structure of the stanza. Two short sentences establish the general rule, set apart grammatically as well as intellectually from the persona's distaste for emotion.

The penultimate verse of the final stanza reiterates the theme of constraint and the structure, by dint of the grammatical isolation of the two ideas, emphasizes this point: "Je sens ou mon pourpoit n'estraint / Chascune vielle [son dueil plaint.]" In a word, the "outer" part of the closing circle represents public opinion, social precepts and the established norm. It is the constraining principle, the "superego," separate from an "inner" reality, divorced from these rules and tenaciously set apart except when the social mores demand a public performance.[5] The grammatical structure, the non-syntactical refrain, in brief, helps to express this conflict within a persona seeking isolation and protection. Form and content interreact to define the psyche of the poetic voice.

What is accomplished by the one line non-syntactical refrain is made more emphatic when the refrain takes up two lines of verse. In Rondeau 150, for example, one encounters once again the refrain which acts as intractable declaration of fact: "Il souffist bien que je le sache, / Sans en enquerir plus avant;" Syntax and textual sign express together resolute withdrawal and self-sufficiency. The second half of the stanza simply restates the case: "Car se tut aloye disant, / On vous pourroit bien dire: attache." The truth about the primacy of self and privacy is stated and then restated. Self remains safely barricaded within the sentence structure and within the protective circle. The analytical perspective is general and not specific. It argues for the right to concealment:

1. Nul de la langue ne m'arrache
   Ce qu'en mon cueur je voys pensant;
2. Il souffist [bien que je le sache,
   Sans en enquerir plus avant.]

It disparages openness and transparency:

Ainsi qu'en blanc pert noire tache,
Vostre fait est si apparant
Que m'y treuve trop cognoissant;
Qui est descouvert, mal se cache:
Il souffist [bien que je le sache.]

The grammatical dynamics are separated from the center, from the enclosed self and the private recesses of the psyche. In that way the form parallels the lexematic message, the enduring theme

---

[5] Lacan's own parallel to the now conventional Freudian triad of Id/Ego/Superego, offers perhaps more lattitude of interpretation: Symbolic Order/Imaginary/Real. For an interesting comparison between the two sets of terms, see the essay by Malcolm Bowie, "Jacques Lacan," in *Structuralism and Since* (Oxford: Oxford University Press, 1970), pp. 32–34.

in the entire opus of Charles d'Orléans, the uncompromising need for isolation from public demands and public leadership.

The ultimate expression of merging form and idea, of syntax and theme underscoring the concept of the "hidden self", is of course the three line refrain. A good example is Rondeau 332 where the poet uses the familiar metaphor of the boat.[6] The first stanza reads:

> Patron vous fays de ma galee,
> Toute chargee de pensee,
> Confort, en qui j'ay ma fiance;

Already the choice of symbol, the enclosed vessel, establishes the psychological theme of protection and isolation. And safe behind the walls of the vessel, safe behind the enclosing lines of this non-syntactical refrain of three lines, is the "chargee de pensee," headed for the "pays de Desirance." At the upper most level of interpretation lies the courtly theme, but at a deeper level is the more important and pervasive idea of the self, encountering the dangers of "la tempeste fortunee / Qui vient du vent de Desplaisance" and demanding a safe journey "Au port de Bonne Destinee." Form and allegorical language reveal the psychological message of fear, fear of exposure and fear of the Other. The voyage of "marchandise d'Esperance" thus requires careful protection, represented first in the symbol of security which is the vessel and then reechoed in the poetic structure itself. In all three stanzas, the three line refrain constitutes a grammatical unit and restates syntactically the theme of isolation by playing upon the rondeau's basic structural circularity.

B. The Incarcerated Self

As in the ballade, however, one also encounters here the interesting paradox of withdrawal as both desirable retreat and unwilling imprisonment, for in spite of the time consuming court

---

[6] For a general analysis of the boat image, see Daniel Poirion, "*La Nef d'Esperance*: Symbole et allégorie chez Charles d'Orléans," in *Mélanges de langue et de littérature du Moyen Age et de la Renaissance offerts à Jean Frappier* (Geneva, Droz, 1970), II: 913–928.

games and the diverse "masks" of distraction, chronic melancholy persists.

In Rondeau 47, the stresses and strains of personal anguish separate the persona from inaccessible happiness. And the syntax itself immediately sets up an adversarial relationship between the harrassed "moi" and the Other, — "sez gens la":

1. Je ne suis pas de sez gens la
   A qui Fortune plaist et rit,
2. De reconfort trop m'escondit,
   Veu que tant de mal donne m'a.

The persona goes on to describe himself as abused and imprisoned by his undefined, and perhaps undefinable misfortunes. What, however, is quite evident, is the willful juxtaposition of psychological truth and fiction, which is incorporated in the syntax:

1. S'on demande comment me va'
   Il est ainsi, comme j'ay dit:
2. Je ne [suis pas de sez gens la
   A qui Fortune plaist et rit]

The intricate psychosyntactical design of the rondeau achieves its fullest expression in the final stanza. Here, not two, but three distinct grammatical units emerge and through their structural relationship duplicate the incarceration topos of the poetic discourse. At one end of the stanza is the voice of the persona, caught during a fleeting moment of optimism and at the other, that same voice, brought back to the harsh reality of despair and gloom. Significantly, within the two grammatical elements is the third, representing the contrasting message of "cueur" who speaks from within the confines of the persona's deeper, wounded self, where the scars of former hurts remain unhealed by either time or courtly pleasures:

1. Quant je dy que bon temps vendra,
   Mon cueur me respont par despit;
2. Voire, s'Espoir ne vous mentit,
   Plusieurs deçoit et decevra.
3. Je ne [suis pas de ses gens la
   A qui Fortune plaist et rit.]

Rondeau 383 is part of a courtly poetic exchange and

therefore more characteristically given over to the uses of allegorical convention. In this instance, syntactical self-sufficiency not only creates a distinct sense of grammatical enclosure, the incarceration theme is built directly into the refrain itself: "Jaulier des prison de Pensee, / Soussy, laissez mon cueur yssir;" Moreover, the poet concretizes his metaphor in the following fashion: "Pasme l'ay veu esvanoir / En la fosse desconfortee," while at the same time, by the grammatical break at the close of the refrain line, he provides a structural mirroring of the basic theme of separation and alienation.

In the second stanza the punctuation suggests a clear copyist's error,[7] for the refrain cannot be construed as appositional to the preceding "vous" which logically must refer rather to "cueur." The enclosure topos thus is retained both lexematically and syntagmatically:

1. [M]ais que seurté vous soit donnee
   De tenir foy et revenir
2. Jaulier [des prisons de Pensee,
   Soussy, laissez mon cueur yssir.]

In the closing stanza of the poem, the refrain is in fact appositional and therefore, in syntactical terms, non-complementary. The circle closes around the prisoner, "cueur," captured by his indefatigable archadversary, "merancolie."

1. [S]'il mouroit en prison fermee,
   Honneur n'y povez acquerir;
2. Veuillez au moins tant l'eslargir
   Qu'ait sa finance pourchassee,
   Jaulier [des prisons de Pensee!]

The close affiliation between lexeme and syntagm make more real the sense of continement. The discursive persona is curiously

---

[7] In recent years several commentators on the Champion edition have raised questions about the transcription of punctuation usage. Jodogne, for example, remarks on a certain inevitable subject of quality in the whole issue of transcribing manuscripts put together by less than conscientious scribes. "Le Rondeau du XVe siècle," p. 401.

entrapped by his own discourse and in spite of what he says, he is his own jailor.

Although we have had occasion to speak of Rondeau 411 in another context, we must return now to the special interplay between form and language. One must once more question, however, the authenticity of the punctuation of the opening stanza, inasmuch as the sense argues for two distinct grammatical units which corroborate each other. The comma at the close of the second line is more logically a period. The two sentences function as syntactical mirrors of the same message, the persona's inescapable anguish characterized as two infinitudes of despair, expressed in both spatial and temporal terms:

1. [C]'est la prison Dedalus
   Que de ma merencollie
2. Quand je la cuide fallie,
   G'i rentre de plus en plus.

The two-line refrain establishes the tone of frustration and suffering which is then syntactically expanded by the parallel sentences.

The mirroring effect of form and content continues into the next stanza where not only does the stanza itself restate the topos as a recurring theme, but grammatically functions in the same way as the opening stanza. It is syntagmatic mirroring of mirroring. Two more sentences, moreover, create a continuing pattern of repeated theme and structure:

1. [A]ucunes foiz, je conclus,
   D'y bouter Plaisance lie;
2. C'est la prison [Dedalus!
   Que de ma merencollie.]

Since it is more probable that the "rentrement," as found here in the final stanza, is more a scribal convention than any true indication of performance practice,[8] the design persists to the end

---

[8] "A Blois le refrain a encore un rôle trop important pour se laisser ramener au simiple *cri*." Poirion, *Le Poète et le prince*, p. 356. "L'erreur qu'on a donc commise est d'avoir mal compris les scribes et les imprimeurs anciens. Dans les rondeaux, ils ont négligé de reproduire chacune des répétitions. Ne faisons-nous

of the rondeau. The basic semiotic plan remains intact as the principle of inescapability is thematically built around the double metaphor of Tantalus and the hermetic life, themselves two faces of the same isotopy of confinement. The syntactical disjunction at the fourth line continues to reinforce in the syntax what is being communicated in the poetic discourse:

1. [O]oncques ne fut Tantalus
   En si trespeneuse vie,
   Ne, quelque chose qu'on die,
   Chartreux, hermite, ou reclus:
2. Cest la prison [Dedalus!].

Because of the inherent characteristics of the rondeau form, the repeated image of imprisonment at the start and again at the end of the poem, firmly implant in the mind of the reader the intended image of enclosing walls, composed, as it were, of verbal stones and syntactical mortar!

Declining health and advancing age add a new dimension to the topos of the imprisoned self. Although the persona is quite capable of donning the various masks of wisdom and philosophical resignation as fruits of his maturer years, the overriding theme of inescapable melancholy remains with him throughout his life.

In the two-part refrain of Rondeau 420, the poetic discourse and syntactical dynamics corroborate each other to express the theme of mortality. Repetition of the substantive "temps" is the lexematic duplication of the chronological prison in which the aging "moi" is entrapped, and whose parameters are the antinomy "Jennesse/Viellesse." The aging, vulnerable persona is thus walled within the inescapable sphere of the unceasing periodicity and redundancy of time, a *temporal* incarceration which represents the human life cycle (circle). That chronological reality is in turn syntagmatically echoed in the enclosure of the non-syntactical refrain. The following two lines of the stanza introduce two more

---

pas comme eux quand nous rappelons le refrain dès le 2e couplet d'une chanson moderne?" Jodogne, "Le Rondeau du XVe siècle," p. 408.

figures in the allegorical drama of life and death, with "moi" caught now between unrelenting "Aage" and unattainable "Liesse":

1. Temps et temps m'ont emblé Jennesse,
   Et laissé es mains de Viellesse
   Ou vois mon pouvre pain querant;
2. Aage ne me veult, tant ne quant,
   Donner l'aumosne de Liesse."

That basic syntactical design is reversed from 3/2 to 2/3 with the refrain serving in the second stanza as the encircling syntagm. The decisive grammatical finality shows this mistress of *time* less bending than the unnamed Woman whose disdain is the commonplace metaphoric displacement for that other psychic reality buried under the poetic discourse of the courtly topos:

1. Puis qu'elle se tient ma maistresse,
   Demander ne luy puis promesse,
   Pour ce, n'enquerons plus avant.
2. Temps [et temps m'ont emblé Jennesse,
   Et laissé es mains de Viellesse.]

In spite of the suspicious comma, the final stanza has an unmistakable tripartite structure, three manifestations of one topos. The allegorical imagery gravitates first toward a concretization in spatial physicality, underscoring the mortality of the persona of flesh and blood who is forever trapped in the human cycle of life and death. While this initial grammatical unit suggests a corporeal incarceration, the second evokes a parallel moral or psychological imprisonment. Here we recognize the self-accusing persona burdened with his own sense of guilt. And in answer to his self-accusatory question, he offers, in a final statement, a response which in Villonesque terms finds some comfort in the undiscriminating, universality of Death:

1. Je n'ay repast que de Foiblesse,
   Couchant sur paille de Destresse,
2. Suy-je bien payé maintenant
   De mes jennes jours cy devant?
3. Nennil, nul n'est qui le redresse:
   Temps et temps [m'ont emblé de Jennesse!]

The topoi of *hidden* or *incarcerated* persona are not distinct, compartmentalized thematic units, but two sides of the same psychological truth. Both themes find corroborative support in the syntactical structure of the rondeau, since both are part of the same general theme of *enclosure*. Indeed, in some important instances, the two seemingly antithetical themes come together, as the reader is made aware of the persona's own ambivalent feelings in this regard.

A good example of how this happens is found in Chanson 82. As is frequently the case, the concreteness of his choice of allegorical metaphor gives to the poet's abstract emotions the sense of palpable reality. In this skillfully wrought piece, he draws from his experience as a hunter to express the feeling of psychological confinement. The hooded ("enchaperonné")[9] hunting bird functions as the lexical displacement for his psychological ambivalence.

In the first stanza, the persona sees himself as a victim of confinement, a confinement which may be increasingly linked to declining health and the resultant libidinal frustrations.[10] In any event, the syntax helps to express the theme of imprisonment and restrictions, whatever their ultimate causes.

The non-syntactical character of the opening refrain dramatizes the assertive and incontrovertible quality of the axiomatic remark. In the second half of the stanza the persona pursues his self-analysis in a statement whose ambiguity calls into question the precise nature of his imprisonment, for, as we have had occasion to point out elsewhere, *Nonchaloir* is both friend and foe, and the withdrawal theme both solace and discomfort. What is not ambivalent, however, is a grammatical structure which forcefully underscores the essential textual sign of isolation. The two recapitulating, non-complementary and self-sufficient sentences strengthen the poetic message of enclosure, communicated here in the image of the grounded bird.

A similar pattern occurs in the second stanza. Two parallel

---

[9] "... comme l'oiseau de chasse au repos à qui on a mis le petit bonnet ou chaperon qui l'aveugle." Champion, *Charles d'Orléans: Poésies*, p. 651.

[10] It is not in the immediate purview of this essay to examine all that may be implied about the persona's sexuality. Suffice it to note quickly that he fathered his first child at age 15 in 1409 and his last at age 58 in 1462.

and mutually reinforcing statements convey the same idea of entrapment behind barriers of syntax, although the text suggests distress rather than comfort. The ambiguity of what the persona feels behind his prison walls and the fact that he is there seem to be two different topological matters:

1. Confort depuis ne lui a
   Cure n'atirer donné.
2. Mon cueur [plus ne volera,
   Il est enchaperonné.]

In the closing stanza the persona returns to the original metaphor to restate his withdrawal from worldly cares in the language of falconry, and once again the syntax plays up the topos of retreat into oneself:

1. Se sa gorge gettera,
   Je ne sçay, car gouverné
   Ne l'ay, mais abandonné;
2. Soit com a venir pourra,
   Mon cueur [plus ne volera!]

In Rondeau 435 the poet uses the refrain structure to create a psychological dichotomy between unattainable pleasure and unavoidable restraints, metonymic statement for the persistent struggle between instinct (Id) and restrictions (Superego). It is in several senses the ultimate statement of the "moi" circumscribed by events. The syntactical arrangement of the opening stanza supports this prevailing ideogram, since the two parts are joined together by the weakest of conjunctions, "et," and are linked thus more by contextual than by syntactical parallelism:

1. Salués moy toute la compaignie
   Ou a present estez a chiere lye
2. Et leur dites que voulentiés seroye
   Avecques eulx, maisestre n'y pourroye,
   Pour Viellesse qui m'a en sa ballie,

Stanza 2 elaborates on the conflictual topos. The sudden syntactical rupture in the second line puts into dramatic relief the clash between what was and what is. Furthermore, the interposed exclamatory, "las," at the middle of the line, forms a psychosemiotic barrier, separating past joy from present disappointment. The concentric circles of enclosure increase as the persona adds another layer born of his own guilt. Finally, contrasting exuberance of the closing refrain emphasizes the delectation from which the "moi" must be excluded, locked behind the prison walls of age and infirmity:

1. Au temps passé, Jennesse sy jolie
   Me gouvernoit; las! or n'y suy ge mye,
   Et pour cela, pour Dieu, que escusé soye;
2. Salueés [moy toute la compaignie
   Ou a present estez a chiere lye.]

The syntagmatic process of layering obstructions which exclude the entrapped persona from the illusive joys of the outside world persists into the final stanza. The theme of a querulous "moi" physically and emotionally incarcerated, finds expression in the contrasting past and present tenses of the main verb "fus" and "suy". Moreover, the ungrammaticality, inverts the structure to place the key word "mye" at the end of the line. This temporal manifestation of alienation is further enhanced by the spatial lexeme "en Paris," as the persona longs for the companionship of friends far away. The inversion of this second half of the syntactical unit is in part the result of homophonic exigencies of the rhyme scheme; but it also serves to create a staccato effect, a jolting movement which, coupled with the strident reiteration of the "i" vowel, emblemizes the nervous discourse of a persona who is imprisoned behind syntagmatic barriers of obstruction.

Then, quite suddenly, in a curious turn-about, the restricting forces of age and time are transferred to the painful demands of life itself. Unexpectedly, the persona admits to having been "sanglé" not by old age and infirmity, but by life. Age and, by implication, Death, is not the persona's jailor but his liberator. What begins as a diatribe against time, turns into a song of freedom, freedom from a world whose restraints and frustrations constitute a strangling bind ("estrete courroye,") from which the incarcerated "moi" must unleash himself!

1. Amoureux fus, or ne le suy ge mye
2. Et en Paris menoye bonne vie;

3. Adieux bon temps, ravoir ne vous saroye!
   4. Bien sanglé fus d'une estrete courroye,
      Que, par Age, convient que la deslie;
   5. Salués moy toute la compaignie!

    Is this a genuine exclamation of joy in deliverance, or yet another mask donned by an adept poetic mime? However one finally interprets the causes of restraint and distress, however one ultimately answers the question of whether the poetic enclosure means protection or incarceration, syntax and textual signs work together as inseparable, interdependent components of the same poetic message.

C. The Interrogative Self

    Another structural technique for enhancing the enclosure motif is the *interrogatio* style,[11] the general effect of which is to deflect attention away from the interrogator, and thus away from the poetic center where the encapsulated persona is situated.

    More than sixty of the rondeaux refrains are of this interrogative type.[12] The interrogative is sometimes the entire refrain line: "Est-ce vers moy qu'envoyez ce souspir?" (51) More frequently it is the whole or a portion of the two-line refrain for which the poet appears to have an increased predilection. The two verse refrain of 610, for example, reads: "A ce jour de Saint Valentin, / Que prandre je, per ou non per?"

    With the longer refrain, of course, the poet has the opportunity for greater complexity and a more varied use of the *interrogatio*. In Rondeau 74 the question takes up only half of the first line: "Cueur, que fais tu? revenge toy / De Soussy et Merencolie." Similarly in Rondeau 220 the question makes up only a small part of the entire refrain: "Que pensé je? dictes moy, / Adevinez, je vous en prye, . . ." In both instances the staccato rhythm suggests

---

[11] This recognized ancient rhetorical device is also often like its corollary, the *ratiocinatio* which is, as Fox succinctly defines it ". . . self-questioning, the achieving of a varied style through the use of rhetorical questions;" *The Lyric Poetry*, p. 93.

[12] See the accompanying appendix for a complete list.

anxiety and apprehension, once again causing text and form to echo each other.

Rondeau 180 achieves the same nervous, jerky effect by the association of explicatives and interrogatives: "A Dieu! qu'il m'anuye, / Helas! qu'esse cy?" Emotional uneasiness is also expressed in Rondeau 300 by the sudden, quick barrage of interrogative pronouns and adverbs: "Qui? quoy? comment? a qui? pourquoy?" followed by a series of expressions of time: "Passez, presens, ou avenir." Thus signifiers and grammatical structure corroborate the pervasive anguish.

Moreover, the *interrogatio* is often extended beyond the opening refrain, adding to the deflective character of the poem and its enclosure motif. In more than one instance, the question form syntactically takes up the entire first stanza:

> Qui est celluy qui s'en tendroit
> De bouter hors Merancolie,
> Quant toute chose reverdie,
> Par les champs, devant ses yeulx, voit? (258)

More than a third of the poetic structure suggests in this way the enclosed persona, a poetic voice communicating through the distancing rhetorical device of the question. The interrogator thus separates himself from the interrogated. He stands apart from his audience, at some safe distance. The psychological implications are clear. In syntactical terms, the question technique reveals the deep-seated anxieties of a persona who wishes to avoid the kind of intimacy which might bring harm, this, in spite of all the pseudo-romantic language of courtly poetry. In a word, one sees here the same insecure persona who has suffered rejection and protects himself behind deflecting syntax, a persona who asks questions of the Other in order perhaps not to have to answer them himself.

But that inevitably leads to an important corollary issue, for who in fact is this Other? Does she or he have a real identity and how does that identity relate to the interrogating self? How specific and "real" the listener is, will have some bearing on how "rhetorical" the question.

For the most part, the audience remains anonymous and

unspecified. Frequently indeed the question appears to be addressed to no one at all or to the world-at-large, as it were.[13]

In Rondeau 60, for example, it is young lovers who are rebuked by an accusatory question: "Que Voulez vous [que plus vous die, / Jeunes assotez amoureux?" In a similarly deprecatory tone, the persona criticizes the "amanz pelerins" in Rondeau 77: "A qui vendez vous voz coquilles?." The following lines, furthermore, make abundantly clear the interrogator's own attitude, for in this case at least he supplies his own response: "Vous cudiez bien, par voz engins, / A tous pertuis trouver chevilles." After all, these pilgrims of love have one thing in mind and the question is asked only to permit the questioner to attack those whom he presumably questions. It is most likely that the antagonistic manner comes in part from the frustrations of declining years, but it is equally true that it comes from the deeper torments of disappointments not-yet-forgotten. In either case, the interrogative form is a syntagmatic expression of a fundamental psychological reality.

Another more complicated example of the *interogatio* is the famous pair of Rondeaux 329–330, in which the questions appear in one rondeau and the answers in the next. Who is this "petit mercier?" Are we to see him as a real person? Does the incident have any reality in the world of experience? These two poems have traditionally been examined from a mimetic / historical perspective.[14] There is, however, much to be gleaned from a more psychological approach to the text. If the poet had written only the first of the two poems then one would be justified in seeing this as yet another example of excluding the Other, of distancing the interrogator from the interrogated. But how does one then explain the response? How does one identify the "petit mercier" who, it

---

[13] 68, 76, 91, 137, 258, 268, 271, 322, 343, 378, 401.
[14] More recently, Alice Planche sees the pair of rondeaux as part of a socio-economic *débat*: "La pensée médiévale est hantée par les confrontations d'allure judiciaire où les opposants se réfèrent à des codes différents: conceptions de l'amour dans le *jeu-parti*, motions du bien et du mal dans le *débat* moral. Les rondeaux CCCXXIX et CCCXXX . . . présentent d'une façon presque théâtrale, le débat du grand et du menu, incarnés par un prince et un mercerot." "Petit mercier, petit panier," in *Mélanges offerts à Pierre Le Gentil*, p. 668.

would appear, has the last word, and a good one at that, a "word" which leaves the interrogator the loser in this verbal confrontation.

There indeed lies the deeper meaning, for the *confrontation* is no more than a device, a clever way in which the persona can play two parts at once and expose in relative safety the double side of his own nature. He is both interrogator and interrogated, not only in the sense that he is the creative persona but in the sense that one side of his psyche identifies with this strong-willed, street vendor, free of the pressures of political and social responsibility, free of the psychological torment of failure. The vendor is the life force (*Eros*) standing firm against that other self-destroying, withdrawing force (*Thanatos*) which forever plagues the persona.[15] The dialogue with "petit mercier," in brief, is just another manifest, discursive transposition of a psychologically latent message, the eternal dialectic between private and public self, between a performing, assertive "moi" and one who is frightened and retiring.

The deflecting interrogative form plays an important role in all the courtly language of love. But out of respect for troubadour traditions, the admired woman necessarily remains unspecified, leaving biographers with the challenging task of identifying the woman being questioned. But these onomastic, if not futile, quests miss the important psychic lesson of the text. Her anonymity serves more than one purpose.

She is asked many questions to which no answer is expected:

Helas! me tuerés vous? (28)
Se vous voulés que tout vostre deviengne? (56)
Mais que vostre cuer soit mien,
Ne doit le mien estre vostre? (207)
En faictes vous doubte? (222)

Whatever the identity of this interrogated person, she is clearly relieved of any need to respond. In the courtly discourse, that silence generally stands for the impatience and determination of the pursuing lover. It may also suggest something about the

---

[15] "Néanmoins nous avons là encore quelques vérités psychologiques à apporter: à savoir combien le prétendu "instinct de conservation" du *moi* fléchit volontiers dans le vertige de la domination de l'espace, . . ." Lacan, *Ecrits*, p. 123.

Male/Female relationship of a society which uses *amours* and its language to perpetuate male domination.[16] Suffice it to say here that the *interrogatio* proves a useful device which leaves the vulnerable "moi" safely protected behind syntactical barriers. It is, in other words, a structural sign representing the persona's own ambiguous emotions toward love, his unbridled desire for acceptance, on the one hand, but also his fears of rejection, on the other.

The only real "naming"which takes place is in the poetic form of allegorical figure, for example: "Fortune" (217, 265), "Merencolie" (266, 286–87), "Saint Valentin" (276, 355), "Traitre Regart" (327), "Soupir" (341), "Esperance" (321), "Penser" (339), "Oeil" (50, 203, 305), and of course, "cueur" (32, 74, 242–3, C 8). More often than not, however, these are mere pantomime figures created, it would seem, in order to listen more than to respond. On occasion, the question serves no purpose beyond mere identification of the other partner:

"Qu'est cela? —C'est Merencolye." (287)
"Qu'esse la? —Qui vient si matin?
—Se suis je. —Vous, Saint Valentin! (355)

On rarer occasions, the interrogation prompts a more elaborate response. In Rondeau 198, one identifies two distinct dialoguists:

Mort de moy! vous y jouez vous?
—En quoy? —Es fais de tromperie.
—Ce n'est que coustume jolie
Dont un peu ont toutez et tous!

In Rondeau 203 "euil" is given an even more active role:

Hau! guette, mon euil! —Et puis quoy?
—Voyez vous riens? Ouyl, assés.
—Qu'est ce? —Cela que vous savez?
Cler, le vous puis moustrer au doy.

By Rondeau 242 a lively verbal match takes place between interrogating persona and responding "Cuer-yeux:"

---

[16] See my "Guillaume d'Aquitaine: Towards a new Paradigmatic Interpretation of 'fin' amors" in *Assays* (Pittsburg, Pa.: University of Pittsburg Press, 1984).

Cuer, qu'esse la? —Ce sommes nous, voz yeux.
—Qu'aportez vous? —Grand foison de nouvelles.
—Quelles sont ilz? —Amoureuses et belles.
—Je n'en vueil point. —Voire? —Non, se m'aist Dieux.

In the following rondeau, the text identifies the participants like *dramatis personnae* in a play and, moreover, transfers the interrogation to one of the two allegorical figures represented:

LE CUEUR. Soussy, beau Sire, je vous prie.
SOUSSY —De quoy? que me demandez vous?
LE CUEUR —Ostez moi d'anuy et courous.
SOUSSY —Ou vous estes? Non feray mie.

One can draw the following conclusion from the analysis of the *interrogatio* form: The question refrain and its occasional extension into the syntax of the first stanza evokes the image of an insulated persona separated from the outside world by poetic structure. Creating a question/answer relationship performs two crucial psychological functions. On the one hand, it deflects the discussion away from the interrogator by burdening the listener with the obligation of a response. On the other hand, it does so by effectively reducing the Other to a silent partner. More often than not therefore dialogue is replaced by monologue, that is, the question either requires no answer or does not allow one. As a result, the persona remains protected by an offensive syntax, one which deprives the listener of retaliation. This silencing technique is in and of itself a communication.[17] It tells us, in a word, how the interrogative style reveals the deeper need for security against potential pain, a security achieved by reducing the Other to a powerless interlocutor.

The personification is of course also a useful technique for self analysis. In the same way that in the ballades "cueur" often functions as an extension of the "moi," here too he is two parts of the same personality, self-critical and self-restrictive. In the above-mentioned Rondeau 242, for example, in which the characters are

---

[17] As Le Galliot notes in defining Lacanian analysis of text: "Car c'est bien une conception duelle qui gouverne la relation analytique, pour laquelle toute parole suppose la possibilité d'une réponse, celle-ci dût-elle se réduire au silence." *Psychanalyse et langages littéraires*, p. 195.

designated like members of a theatrical production, it is "Cueur" who prompts action and the other self who opts for withdrawal. The psychological signification is twofold. The fragmentation represents the Freudian dichotomy of a more aggressive, assertive self (Id), restricted by a more cautious, anxious self (Superego). It also signifies the well-established pattern of a fearful "moi" who separates the more visible, inquiring persona, from the more private and pained persona in order to maintain protective separation from any repressed, inner trauma. The designation, thus, of a separate though silenced interlocutor, continues to function as a psychically distancing device.

In either case, the interrogative form is another syntagmatic phenomenon whose psychological implications are parallel to all that has already been observed about the insecure, wounded self. This cautious persona seeks to achieve release of frustration, but always at a safe distance.

* * * *

In the inherent circularity of the rondeau, the topos of deflection/reflection finds a perfect poetic vehicle for a new brand of lyricism which is characterized by patterns of psychological paradox. The careful manipulation of non-syntactical refrains and the *interrogatio* form enhance the idea of enclosure which suggests at one and the same time protection and incarceration.

In one important psychosemiotic interpretation of the text, the fragile self can be seen as taking refuge in the deflective experience of poetic expression. Moreover, even as he performs, he remains paradoxically at a safe distance from public scrutiny. At another level of meaning, the withdrawing, reflective self discovers, alongside deep-rooted traumas, a growing uneasiness about old age and death. In a final paradoxical posture, the persona appears to reverse the scheme of things by defining not death but life as the ultimate incarceration. The Death instinct, (Thanatos), in other words, seems to triumph over the Life instinct (Eros).

Conclusion
Signification

> Chacun devise a son propos,
> Quant a moy, je suis loing du mien.
> (Rondeau 233)

Text is the crossroads where persona and reader meet. In normal discourse the interlocutor is separated from *intended* (manifest) meaning by the speaker's signifying symbols. But language provides access not only to an intended message but to the unintential (latent) meaning buried at the unconscious level. Discourse, in other words, creates a cycle of communication which begins with the discursive persona, working through the signifying symbols, to the reader, and then back again to the unconsciously discursive persona who exists behind the manifest discourse.

That principle has always been at the core of psychotextual analysis. Less apparent as a source of meaning, however, are the syntactical elements of the text. Yet they are just as much a part of the speaker's communication. Indeed, the task of the interpreter decoding poetic discourse, must necessarily include syntagmatic as well as lexematic signs in order to arrive at the complete signification of the text at both its manifest and latent levels of meaning.

Complicating the process of interpretation is the whole

issue of poetic language, and in the case of Charles d'Orléans, the uses of the courtly allegorical mode of expression. Whereas in normal discourse the signifier has an essentially denotative function, the language of poetry in general, and that of allegory in particular, is more often connotative in nature. It is crucial thus to any psychosemiotic examination of the Charles d'Orléans text to understand the role of personification, for it is a key factor in defining the "lyric" qualities of the message and in identifying the persona behind them.

Through the personifying device of abstraction, the poet aims at concreteness.[1] This allegorical concretization of emotion normally creates another degree of distance between symbol and signification. But paradoxically, it is this very phenomenon which establishes an important *psychological* link between objectivized idea and objectivizer. The courtly idiom becomes a convenient metaphoric displacement whose symbolic language is at one and the same time the persona's vehicle for analyzing self at a seemingly safe distance, and the reader's access into the latent content of his message.

> [La technique psychologique] rend moins désuet l'usage des métaphores et des allégories comme moyen de définition et d'approche d'une réalité qui échappe à l'analyse logique."[2]

And what in fact does this once-removed, auto-analysis reveal? A careful reading of both syntagmatic and lexematic signs uncovers a persona torn between private and public self, a persona who seeks asylum from both the fear of new hurts and the recollection of old ones. There is thus a psychological balancing of introversion and extroversion, an alternating *deflecting* and *reflecting* mood. The traumatized "moi" who has suffered physical incarceration experiences a more profound and chronic imprisonment engendered not only by hurts from without but by anxieties from within. The nervous, fragile persona who has endured the

---

[1] "Charles d'Orléans convoque aussi dans son univers imaginaire ces figures idéales qui caractérisent la tradition courtoise à l'aube du XVe siècle. Mais l'allégorie chez lui serre la réalité de près." Poirion, *Le Poète et le prince*, p. 541.

[2] Planche, *Charles d'Orléans ou à la recherche d'un langage*, p. 728.

pain of rejection retreats from the world but also longs for assurances of loyalty and affection. This psychic paradox is expressed through the allegorical idiom. Self torments self with fears (SOUCCY/ENNUY) of disapprobation (DOLEUR, DESTRESS). The delicate and apprehensive persona frets over potential loyalty (FAULCETE), born of hypocrisy (MAINTIEN HONTEUX) and threatening enemies (DANGIER). He withdraws thus into a protective enclosure of his inner self (CHAMBRE DE PENSEE), where, however, he encounters the memory of former wounds.

To deal effectively with this dilemma, he makes use of several psychopoetic devices. He creates, first, an alter ego, a "Cueur" which allows him to maintain a safe distance from the distress he must describe. He hides behind allegorical masks, the most familiar of which is *Nonchalance*, a kind of philosophical indifference which increases with advancing old age. He also uses the pyrotechnics of courtly language which, pushed to its farthest limits, turns *écriture* into another masking device.

The syntactical dynamics corroborate this psycholiterary phenomenon. Although the preceding analysis treats only the refrain, the structural patterns are clear and decisive. The dynamics of the ballade refrain emblemize the idiolect of a self-encapusulating "moi" hiding simultaneously from external and internal peril, from that *Autre* who seems to intrude both from within and without.[3] In the rondeau, the inherent circularity of the form dramatically underscores that psychological effect. The non-syntactical refrain and the *interrogatio* form, both accentuate the enclosure topos, leaving the reader with the unmistakable sense of an anxious self, as much afraid of the world, as needing it, as much afraid of privacy, as requiring it—in a word, a poetic discourse fraught with paradox.

To begin with, deflection and reflection represent two sides of the same psychic need. The persona deflects *away* from self in

---

[3] "More consistently than any other of Lacan's terms 'the Other' refuses to yield a single sense; in each of its incarnations it is that which introduces 'lack' and 'gap' into the operations of the subject and which, in doing so, incapacitates the subject for selfhood, or inwardness, or apperception, or plenitude; it guarantees the indestructibility of desire by keeping the goals of desire in perpetual flight." Malcolm Bowie, "Jacques Lacan," in *Structuralism and Since*, p. 134.

order to preserve his privacy. But within that paradoxical phenomenon is yet another, for in reflecting, he learns that he must also deflect away from self in order to avoid confrontation with former psychological wounds. Moreover, the metaphoric language behind which he hides provides access into his deeper psychic self. *Ecriture* thus represents both withdrawal (*Thanatos*) and recognition (*Eros*), protection and incarceration, concealment and exposure.

In brief, the curious phenomenon of the "lyric" qualities of Charles d'Orléans' poetry resides in these paradoxical psychopoetic patterns in which concrete abstraction becomes abstract concreteness, *en*closure, *dis*closure, *de*flection, *re*flection and the mask, a discovery of the hidden self. Both textual signs and syntactical dynamics bring his reader closer thus to a persona who no doubt describes far more than he ever intended.

Appendix A
Ballade Refrain

Ballade	Grammatical Classification	Lines Per Stanza	# of Syntactical Lines of Refrain Per Stanza
1	conj	8	7/7/2
2	app	8	6/2/8
3	comp	10	2/2/2
4	n-s	7	
5	comp	9	5/4/3
6	n-s	9	
7	comp	9	5/5/3
8	n-s	8	
9	n-s	9	
10	conj	8	4/2/8
11	comp	11	10/4/4
12	comp	8	8/3/6
13	conj	9	5/2/5
14	comp	9	2/1/1
15	comp	8	5/8/4
16	comp	8	6/4/2
17	comp	9	9/4/5
18	comp	8	8/2/2
19	comp	8	3/2/4
20	comp	10	4/2/10
21	comp	10	6/3/5
22	app	8	8/3/4
23	n-s	8	

24	comp	8	6/2/8
25	n-s	8	
26	n-s	9	
27	comp	9	9/2/3
28	conj	11	7/5/6
29	conj	8	2/2/2
30	conj	9	5/2/3
31	conj	8	3/8/4
32	comp	8	8/5/3
33	comp	8	2/2/2
34	comp	8	3/4/4
35	comp	9	2/2/6
36	comp	8	4/4/2
37	comp	9	4/4/2
38	conj	11	2/2/6
39	comp	9	9/3/7
40	n-s	10	
41	n-s	8	
42	comp	11	2/5/2
43	n-s	11	
44	conj	15	3/3/6
45	comp	8	3/3/4
46	comp	8	6/6/6
47	comp	9	1/1/1
48	comp	8	3/4/3
49	comp	8	6/2/2
50		8	2/1/4
51	n-s	10	
52	conj	9	2/2/1
53	comp	8	2/2/1
54	app	10	6/3/2/5/5
55	conj	9	3/4/2
56		10	1/1/1
57	comp	9	5/3/2
58	conj	9	2/2/3
59	n-s	8	
60	comp	8	8/2/2/5
61	conj	11	2/3/5
62		10	1/2/1
63	comp	8	4/2/6
64	comp	8	2/3/4
65	conj	9	5/4/2
66	comp	8	4/2/4

67	comp	11	2/2/2
68	comp	8	3/2/2
69	comp	11	1/5/2/3
70	comp	9	5/2/2
71	comp	9	5/7/3
72	comp	11	4/3/4
73	comp	7	2/5/7/2
74	n-s	8	
75	comp	7	3/2/2
76	n-s	10	
77	comp	10	10/4/3
78	comp	8	8/2/5/2
79	n-s	8	
80	comp	8	4/3/3
81	comp	11	5/6/2
82	comp	9	2/3/3
83	n-s	8	
84	comp	8	4/2/4
85	comp	10	2/2/2
86		8	2/5/2
87	conj	8	2/2/2
88	comp	11	7/2/3
89	comp	8	8/5/3
90	comp	7	3/2/2
91	n-s	7	
92	comp	8	2/2/5
93		8	2/4/4
94	comp	8	4/4/4
95	comp	7	2/5/2/3
96	conj	8	6/2/4
97		8	3/4/8/1/5/4
98	comp	8	8/5/2
99	comp	8	2/4/8
100	comp	7	2/2/2
101	conj	11	2/2/2
102	comp	8	4/2/2
103	conj	11	8/4/4
104	comp	7	3/5/7
105	comp	9	2/3/5
106		8	2/2/5/3
107	comp	8	2/1/5/3
108	n-s	8	
109	comp	8	4/8/4

110	conj	9	3/3/5
111	comp	8	8/8/8
112	comp	8	8/4/4
113	comp	9	4/4/3
114	comp	9	1/5/2/3
115	comp	9	2/2/1
116			
117	csomp	8	8/3/3
118	comp	8	8/3/2
119	comp	8	4/4/4
120		7	3/2/5
121	conj	7	3/2/5
122	comp	9	5/4/5
123	conj	8	4/2/3

Appendix B
Rondeau Refrain

One line:

    1–9, 11–45, 49–51, 56, 58–59, 61–63, 68–69, 90, 112–119, 121–123, 140, 164, 177, 224, 228, 254, 256, 261, 264, 272–273, 275, 281–282, 323, 330, 339, 352, 355, 358–359, 361, 370, 398, 431

Two lines:

    10, 46–48, 52–55, 57, 60, 64–67, 70–81, 84–89, 91–111, 120–124, 126, 132, 142–163, 165, 166–174, 175–176, 178–197, 198, 199–204, 206–211, 213, 215, 217–224, 229, 231–238, 241–245, 247–249, 251, 257–260, 262–269, 265–271, 274, 276, 283, 285–307, 310–322, 324–326, 331, 334–337, 341–343, 346–349, 351, 354, 356, 364–365, 367–368, 374, 377–383, 390–392, 394–395, 397, 400, 402–404, 406, 410–411, 420–424, 427–428, 432–433, 435

Three lines:

    83, 280, 327–329, 332, 338, 375–376, 396, 401, 425, 434

Non-syntactical:

    12, 14, 24, 28–32, 35, 41–43, 47, 51–56, 60, 63, 65–66, 68–69, 71, 73–74, 76–77, 79, 81, 83–84, 87–88, 90–92, 95–96, 100–101, 104, 123–124, 126, 128, 132, 142, 144, 146–147, 149–154, 158–160, 162–163, 166–169, 171, 173, 178–180. 183–191, 193–201, 203, 206–208, 215, 217–221, 224, 231–238, 241–243, 245, 247–248, 256, 258–260, 262, 264–267, 269–273, 276, 284, 288–294, 296, 298, 300–302, 304, 306–307, 310, 312, 314–315, 319–322, 326–327,

329, 332–333, 339–340, 343, 347–349, 351, 355–356, 364–366, 370, 377–378, 382–387, 391, 400–401, 403, 406, 410–411, 415, 420, 424–425, 427, 431–435

Syntactical:

Appositional:

4, 330, 336, 361, 397

Conjunctional:

9, 18, 23, 38, 45, 49, 58, 64, 74, 98, 120, 143–144, 157, 170, 190, 213, 229, 244, 280–282, 297, 303, 328, 334, 338, 346, 358–359, 390

Complementary:

1, 3, 6–8, 16, 19, 21, 25–26, 30, 34, 36–37, 39–40, 44, 46, 48, 50, 57, 59, 61–62, 70, 75, 78, 80, 82, 85–86, 89, 93, 109–110, 114, 118–119, 121, 125, 140, 148, 151, 155–156, 161, 164–165, 172, 174, 176–177, 181, 204, 209–211, 225, 228, 235, 249–250 254, 257, 261, 268, 274–275, 283, 285, 295, 305, 311, 313, 317–318, 324–325, 331, 337, 342, 352, 354, 358, 368, 374–375, 379–381, 399, 402, 421–422, 428

Selected Bibliography

The following titles represent only those materials which appear in either the body of the text or in the footnotes. For more complete bibliographical information on Charles d'Orléans, the reader is advised to consult the extensive lists in Fein, Planche and Poirion, and, for further reading on the relationship between psychology and literature, the bibliographical lists provided by Le Galliot, Strelka and Tytell.

Bowie, Malcolm. "Jacques Lacan." In *Structuralism and Since*. Oxford: University Press, 1970.

Charles d'Orléans. *Poésies*. Edited by Pierre Champion. 2 vols. 1923–27. Reprint. Paris: Honoré Champion, 1965.

Cholakian, Rouben. "Guillaume d'Aquitaine: Towards a New Paradigmatic Interpretation of *fin'amors*" In *Assays* Pittsburg, Pa.: Pittsburg University Press, 1984.

Cigado, Sergio. *L'Opera poetica di Charles d'Orléans* Milano: Vita et Pensiero, 1960.

Dragonetti, Roger. *La Technique poétique des trouvères dans la chanson courtoise* Bruges: De Tempel, 1960.

Fein, David. *Charles d'Orléans*. Boston: Twayne, 1983.

―――. "Verb Usage in a Ballad of Charles d'Orléans." *Romance Philology* 35 (November: 1981).

Fox, John. *The Lyric Poetry of Charles d'Orléans*. Oxford, Clarendon Press, 1969.

Freud, Sigmund. *The Interpretation of Dreams*. Translated by A. A. Brill, New York: Macmillan, 1913.

―――. *Ma Vie et la psychanalyse* Paris: Gallimard, 1958.

Goodrich, N. L. *Charles d'Orléans: A Study of Themes in His French and in His English Poetry.* Geneva: Droz, 1967.

Gennrich, Fr. *Grundriss einer Formenlehre des mittelalterlichen Liedes als Grundlage einer musikalischer Formenlehre des Liedes.* Halle: Saale, 1932.

Grévisse, Maurice. *Précis de grammaire française.* 26th rev. ed. Gembloux; Duculot, 1957.

Harrison, Anne Tukey. *Charles d'Orléans and the Allegorical Mode.* Chapel Hill: University of North Carolina Press, 1975.

Holmes, U. T. and Alexander Schutz. *A History of the French Language.* Columbia, Ohio: Harold Hedrick, 1948.

Jodogne, Omer. "Le Rondeau du XVe siècle mal compris. Du dit et de l'écrit." In *Mélanges de langue et de littérature médiévales offerts à Pierre le Gentil.* Paris: S. E. D. E. S., 1973.

Jung, C. G. *The Portable Jung* New York: Penguin Press, 1976.

Jakobson, Roman. *Essai de linguistique générale.* Paris: Seuil, 1963.

Kristeva, Julia. *Séméiotiké: recherches pour une sémioanalyse.* Paris: Seuil, 1966.

Lacan, Jacques. *Ecrits.* Paris: Seuil, 1966.

Le Galliot, J. *Psychanalyse et le langage littéraire.* Paris: F. Nathan, 1977.

Lote, George. *Histoire du vers français.* 3 vols. Paris: Boivin, 1949–55.

Newman, Karen. "The Mind's Castle: Containment in the Poetry of Charles d'Orléans." *Romance Philology.* 33 (1979): 317–28.

Paris, Jean. "The Mortal Sign: Psychological Implications of Linguistic Elements in Literature." Translated by Daniel A Brewer. In *Literary Criticism and Psychology.* Edited by Joseph P. Strelka. Pennsylvania Park, Penn: Pennsylvania State University Press, 1976.

Pasquali, Constanza. "Charles d'Orléans e il suo 'Nonchaloir.' " In *Studi in onore di Angelo Monteverdi.* Modena: 1959.

Planche, Alice. *Charles d'Orléans ou à la recherche d'un langage.* Paris: Honoré Champion, 1975.

———. "Petit Mercier, petit panier." In *Mélanges de langue et de litérature médiévales offerts à Pierre Le Gentil.*Paris: S. E. D. E. S., 1973.

Poirion, Daniel. *Le Lexique de Charles d'Orléans dans les ballades.* Geneva: Droz, 1967.

———. *Le Poète et le prince: l'évolution du lyrisme courtois de Guillaume de Machaut à Charles d'Orléans* Paris: Presses universitaires de France, 1965.

———."*La Nef d'Espérance*: Symbole et allégorie chez Charles d'Orléans," In *Mélanges de langue et de littérature du moyen age et de la renaissance offerts à Jean Frappier* Geneva: Droz, 1970.

Reaney, Gilbert. "Concerning the Origins of the Rondeau, Virelai and Ballade Forms. "*Musica Disciplina.* 6 (1952): 155–166.

Sasaki, Shegemi. *Sur le Thème de nonchaloir dans la poésie de Charles d'Orléans.* Paris: Nizet, 1974.

Spanke, Hans. *Beziehungen zwischen romanischer und mittellateinischer Lyrik mit besonderer Berüchsichtigung des Metrik und Musik.* Berlin: Abhandlung des Gessellschaft des Wissenschaft zu Göttingen, 1936.

Tytell, Pamela. *La Plume sur le divan: Psychanalyse et littérature en France.* Paris: Aubier Montaigne, 1982.

Starobinsky, Jean. "L'Encre de la mélancolie." *Nouvelle Revue française.* 123 (1963): 410–423.

Watson, Harold. "Charles d'Orléans: 1394–1465." *Romanic Review* 61 (February: 1965):3–11.

Zumthor, Paul. "Charles d'Orléans et le langage de l'allégorie." In *Mélanges offertes à Ritu Lejeune.* 2 vols. Gembloux. J. Duculot, 1969.

———. *Essai de poésie médiévale.* Paris: Seuil, 1972.

Scripta humanistica

Published Volumes

D. W. McPheeters, *Estudios humanísticos sobre la "Celestina."* $24.50.

Everett W. Hesse, *The "Comedia" and Points of View.* $24.50.

Marta Ana Diz, *Patronio y Lucanor: la lectura inteligente "en el tiempo que es turbio."* Prólogo de John Esten Keller. $26.00.

Estudios literarios en honor de Gustavo Correa. Eds. Manuel Durán, Charles Faulhaber, Richard Kinkade, T. A. Perry. $25.00.

Francisco Delicado, *Portrait of Lozana: The Exuberant Andalusian Woman.* Translation, introduction and notes by Bruno M. Damiani. $33.00.

Renaissance and Golden Age Studies in Honor of D. W. McPheeters. Ed. Bruno M. Damiani. $25.00.

James F. Jones, Jr., *The Story of a Fair Greek of Yesteryear.* A Translation from the French of Antoine-François Prévost's *L'Histoire d'une Grecque moderne.* With Introduction and Selected Bibliography. $30.00.

Colette H. Winn, *Jean de Sponde: Les sonnets de la mort ou La poétique de l'accoutumance.* Préface par Frédéric Deloffre. $22.50.

Paul A. Gaeng, *Collapse and Reorganization of the Latin Nominal Flection as Reflected in Epigraphic Sources*. Written with the assistance of Jeffrey T. Chamberlin. $24.00.

Salvatore Calomino, *From Verse to Prose: The Barlaam and Josaphat Legend in Fifteenth-Century Germany*. $28.00.

Jack Weiner, *"En busca de la justicia social: estudio sobre el teatro español del Siglo de oro,"* $24.50.

Edna Aizenberg, *The Aleph Weaver: Biblical, Kabbalistic and Judaic Elements in Borges*. $25.00.

Michael G. Paulson and Tamara Alvarez-Detrell, *Cervantes, Hardy, and "La fuerza de la sangre."* $25.50.

Rouben Charles Cholakian, *Deflection/Reflection in the Lyric Poetry of Charles d'Orleans*. $22.50.

Forthcoming

Carlo Di Maio, *Antifeminism in Selected Works of Enrique Jardiel Poncela*. $20.50.

Philip J. Spartano, *Giacomo Zanella: Poet, Essayist, and Critic of the "Risorgimento."* Preface by Roberto Severino. $24.00.

Juan de Mena, *Coplas de los siete pecados mortales: Second and Third Continuations*. Ed. Gladys Rivera. $25.50.

Barbara Mujica, *Spanish Pastoral Characters*. $25.00.

Susana Hernández Araico, *La ironía en tragedias de Calderón*. $25.00.

Kent Ljungquist, *The Grand and the Fair: Poe's Landscape Aesthetics and Pictorial Techniques*. $25.00.

Vittorio Felaco, *The Poetry and Selected Prose of Camillo Sbarbaro*. Edited and Translated by Vittorio Felaco. With a Preface by Franco Fido. $25.00.